Moore College School of Theology 2015

'Tend My Sheep'

The word of God and pastoral ministry

Editor: Keith Condie

The Latimer Trust

ISBN 978-1-906327-44-6

Cover photo: Shepherds and sheep Carpathians© panaramka –fotolia.com

Published by the Latimer Trust September 2016

The Latimer Trust (formerly Latimer House, Oxford) is a conservative Evangelical research organisation within the Church of England, whose main aim is to promote the history and theology of Anglicanism as understood by those in the Reformed tradition. Interested readers are welcome to consult its website for further details of its many activities.

The Latimer Trust
London N14 4PS UK
Registered Charity: 1084337
Company Number: 4104465
Web: www.latimertrust.org
E-mail: administrator@latimertrust.org

CONTENTS

Preface

To oversee Christ's flock is 'a noble task' (1 Timothy 3:1) but also a difficult task. The responsibilities and expectations of the job are numerous and weighty. Skills in leadership and management, the ability to communicate effectively in a variety of settings, the need to be a competent listener and counsellor – these things and more are required of those who exercise pastoral oversight, even of a small congregation. And as pastors seek resources to assist them in their vocation, it is no wonder that many have drawn upon and found great benefit from the insights of the social sciences. The problem, however, is that in so doing it is possible to be drawn away from the core business of the pastoral task, i.e., the ministry of the word of God that proclaims the gospel of the Lord Jesus Christ. Andrew Purves believes 'that something has gone seriously awry' in much contemporary ministry practice. 'My broad concern', he states, 'is the seeming lack of connection between exegesis of the Scriptures and the central Christian doctrines, on the one hand, and the theology and practice of ministry today, on the other.'

The chapters that follow do not claim to offer an extensive critique or response to this issue. Rather, each is written from the perspective that authentic pastoral ministry is grounded in the ministry of the word of God. The authors turn to Scripture for an understanding of the nature and purpose of ministry, and in so doing, seek to build confidence that word-based ministry lies at the heart of God's means to bring about His good purposes in this world. Each chapter was first delivered as a lecture at the 2015 School of Theology held at Moore Theological College.

The volume opens with Lionel Windsor's careful investigation of the meaning of the phrase 'the work of ministry' in Ephesians 4:12. Drawing upon the work of John Collins, he demonstrates that the oft-quoted statement that 'ministry' means 'service' is inaccurate, and that in the letter to the Ephesians the word carries the idea of bringing God's revelation to people. Furthermore, he argues that it is 'the saints' who do 'the work of ministry' and that these 'saints' are the Jewish Christians that comprised the very early stages of the church in Ephesus. The ministry to which these believers were called was to bring the heavenly gospel of Christ to the nations, a task still relevant to Christians today.

In chapter 2 Mark Thompson turns our attention to a key Protestant conviction, the doctrine of the sufficiency of Scripture. Noting that 'sufficient' is an incomplete predicate, he asks, 'sufficient for what?' In dialogue with the likes of early orthodox theologians François Turretin and Benedict Pictet, he argues that the doctrine does not mean that the Bible tell us everything about everything. Yet neither can we allow for an error in the opposite direction, i.e. to think that the Scriptures can be relativised in a manner that undercuts their distinctive character as God-breathed. Two test cases – preaching and pastoral counselling – flesh out the implications of his discussion. While noting that it is possible to attempt to use Scripture in ways not intended by its divine author, our fundamental response ought to be robust confidence in God's provision for his people in his written word.

In the third chapter David Peterson wrestles with the question of what pastoral preaching looks like. He considers the New Testament evidence concerning Paul's ministry to the church in Ephesus and notes that the apostle's preaching involved an ongoing exposition of the gospel and its implications. If application of the word of God today is not to be simplistic, not only will the structure and theology of the biblical passage need to be carefully analysed, but the preacher will also need to have a thorough understanding of those being addressed. Pastoral preaching will always be seeking to move beyond simply conveying the content of the text to teasing out its relevance and significance for the intended audience. It will speak to hearers holistically, engaging mind, will and emotions in a manner that sees lives changed for God's glory.

Next, Peter Orr provides another detailed exegetical study, this time of 2 Corinthians 1:3-7 and its dominant motif of 'comfort'. It is argued that because Isaiah 40–66 provides the background to the apostle Paul's usage of the term, 'comfort' must be closely linked with salvation. Comfort comes as the word of God is appropriately spoken to those suffering affliction of some kind. As that word is believed, the afflicted are enabled to persevere and take hold of the salvation that is theirs in Christ. Christian leaders today are to call people to follow the example of Paul who was prepared to share in the sufferings of Christ, but who, in so doing, received the very comfort of Christ.

Finally, Keith Condie provides a case study of a ministry centred on the word of God – that of the seventeenth-century English Puritan, Richard Baxter. Baxter believed that pastoral oversight was such a high calling that only those who were attentive to their own spiritual condition could be human instruments to effect reformation in others. Faithful ministry also entailed certain key priorities – drawing people to faith and spiritual maturity through individual catechising as well as accessible preaching, exercising church discipline, and uniting with other pastors in the cause of the gospel. While certain emphases of his ministry are open to critique, there is much in his approach that is suggestive for contemporary pastoral work.

Our hope is that these chapters will encourage pastors and others in their confidence that it is the word of God's grace that builds Christ's church and enables individual believers to grow in maturity.

Keith Condie

Contributors

Keith Condie is Co-Director of the Mental Health and Pastoral Care Institute, Anglican Deaconess Ministries, Sydney. Previously he was Dean of Students and Lecturer in Ministry and Church History at Moore Theological College.

Peter Orr has taught New Testament at Moore Theological College since 2014. Prior to that he taught New Testament at Melbourne School of Theology. His research interests include New Testament Christology and his volume *Christ Absent and Present: A Study in Pauline Christology* was published in 2014.

David Peterson is an emeritus faculty member at Moore Theological College, where he continues to teach part time. He is a co-founder of Cornhill Sydney, where he pursues his passion to develop effective biblical preachers. His most recent publications include *The Acts of the Apostles* (PNTC), *Transformed by God* (Inter-Varsity Press), and *Encountering God Together* (Inter-Varsity Press).

Mark D Thompson is the Principal and Head of Theology at Moore Theological College, Sydney. He is the author of numerous articles and books, and has a particular interest in the doctrines of Scripture, the Trinity, Christ, and Justification by Faith.

Lionel Windsor is an Anglican Minister in the Diocese of Sydney currently serving as New Testament Lecturer at Moore Theological College. He graduated from Moore in 2005 (BD) and from Durham University in 2012 (PhD). He is the author of a number of scholarly and popular works, with a special interest in biblical theology and its relation to Christian ministry.

1. The Work of Ministry in Ephesians 4:12 – *Lionel Windsor*

Ephesians 4:11-12 is a foundational and often-cited text in relation to pastoral ministry:

> And he [Christ] gave the apostles, the prophets, the evangelists, the shepherds and teachers, to equip the saints for the work of ministry, for building up the body of Christ, ... (Ephesians 4:11-12, *ESV*)

The focus of this essay is on the phrase, 'the work of ministry' (verse 12). What exactly is this work of ministry? The question has been posed and answered at many times and in various ways. Our aims here are, firstly, to seek some biblical precision and clarity on this phrase, and secondly, to draw out some implications for pastoral ministry today.

1.1. *Ministry means 'service'?*

Ephesians 4:12 is frequently brought in to discussions about the *status* of those in formal ministry roles. This is an issue that can often become problematic. In previous generations, the problem expressed itself in clericalism;[1] more recently it has surfaced in the over-professionalisation of pastoral roles[2] and the phenomenon of the 'celebrity' pastor or preacher.[3] This problem is frequently countered by the use of a simple slogan: 'Ministry means service'.[4] The slogan is meant to imply that ministerial pride is absurd. Because the biblical word 'ministry' (διακονία) itself is fundamentally about serving, and therefore about being humble, there is absolutely no room for ministers to be proud, to feel privileged or to over-professionalise their role.

---

1 Markus Barth, *Ephesians*, 2 vols., *The Anchor Bible* 34, 34A (Garden City: Doubleday, 1974), pp 477-484.

2 For a discussion of the problem in general see John Piper, *Brothers, We Are Not Professionals: A Plea to Pastors for Radical Ministry*, 2nd ed. (Nashville: Broadman & Holman, 2013).

3 Rachel Held Evans, 'When Jesus Meets TMZ: Why Celebrity Culture Is Overtaking Our Pulpits,' *Relevant Magazine*, February 9, 2012, http://www.relevantmagazine.com/god/church/features/28236-when-jesus-meets-tmz.

4 E.g. 'In the Bible, the word "ministry" means "service"': *Full-Time Paid Ministry in the Diocese of Sydney*, (Sydney: Anglican Church Diocese of Sydney Department of Ministry Training & Development, 2nd ed. 2009), p 6.

Ministers are, by definition, merely servants of others. Thus ministerial pride is, quite literally, a contradiction in terms.

The simplicity and effectiveness of this lexical claim cannot be denied. It nips in the bud any notion that ministry is a career or a way to secure one's place in the world. However, is the lexical claim *true*? In the Bible, does the word 'ministry' really mean 'service'?

1.2. *The history of the claim*

In 1990, John Collins, lecturer in theology and history at the Melbourne College of Divinity, published a book titled after the Greek word: *Diakonia*.[5] In his book, Collins thoroughly re-examined the Greek sources, and came to some significant and far-reaching conclusions regarding the meaning of the term.

1.2.1. *Origins*

According to Collins, the idea that the word διακονία *essentially* means 'humble, loving service' can be traced to the Lutheran churchmen of nineteenth-century Germany.[6] In the face of modern trends towards urbanisation and industrialisation, a pressing need arose to care for the large numbers of displaced weak, sick, needy and suffering German people.[7] A diaconal movement arose to carry out this task. The movement was undergirded by the claim that διακονία referred to the kind of loving, humble service exemplified by its members. In 1935, the claim gained great theological and exegetical *gravitas* when it was incorporated into the article on διακονία and its cognates in Kittel's famous *Theological Dictionary of the New Testament (TDNT)*.[8] The article is at pains to

---

5 John N Collins, *Diakonia: Re-Interpreting the Ancient Sources* (Oxford: Oxford University Press, 1990).

6 Collins, *Diakonia*, pp 8-11.

7 Cf. Kari Latvus, 'The Paradigm Challenged: A New Analysis of the Origin of Diakonia,' *Stud. Theol.* 62, no. 2 (2008): pp 142-143.

8 Hermann W Beyer, 'διακονέω, διακονία, διάκονος,' ed. Gerhard Kittel, *Theologisches Wörterbuch Zum Neuen Testament* (Stuttgart: Kohlhammer, 1935), pp 81-93; ET trans. Geoffrey W Bromiley, *Theological Dictionary of the New Testament* (Grand Rapids: Eerdmans, 1964), pp 81-93. Beyer relied heavily on the work of Brandt whose monograph had connected διάκονος / διακονία with the ideals of the Lutheran diaconate (Collins, *Diakonia*, p 11). For a further instance of theological presuppositions affecting semantic analysis in the TDNT (in this instance Klaus Wegenast's article on the term διδάσκω) see Claire S Smith, 'Unchanged "Teaching": The Meaning of *Didaskō* in 1 Timothy 2:12,' in *Women, Sermons and the Bible: Essays Interacting with John Dickson's Hearing Her Voice*, ed. Peter G Bolt and Tony Payne (Sydney: Matthias Media, 2014), Kindle, § 3.a.iv.

emphasise the humble, servile nature of the word-group. It claims that the secular Greek verb διακονέω fundamentally meant 'to wait at table'.[9] This table-service was the 'original concrete sense which is still echoed in its figurative meanings'.[10] The article argues that early Christians took this basic secular meaning – waiting at tables – and transformed it into a general mindset involving humble service towards one's neighbour. Thus 'to minister' in the New Testament refers to 'any "discharge of service" in genuine love.'[11] So in Ephesians 4:12, the word διακονία means 'all significant activity for the edification of the community.'[12]

1.2.2. *Influence*

This idea that διακονία essentially means 'humble service' has been highly influential in New Testament studies and beyond.[13] It is often used to draw implications concerning the nature of 'ministry' today.

For example, the *New International Dictionary of New Testament Theology* follows the *TDNT* closely: it argues that the word 'ministry' in Ephesians 4:12 means 'all services in the Christian community.'[14]

Eduard Schweizer, writing in 1971 about the significance of the term διακονία for church offices, states:

> Thus the New Testament throughout and uniformly chooses a word that is entirely unbiblical and non-religious and never includes association with a particular dignity or position ... In the development of Greek the basic meaning, 'to serve at table,' was extended to include the more comprehensive idea of 'serving.' It nearly always denotes something of inferior value ... The New

9 LXX usage of the term is negligible. The verb διακονέω is absent altogether from the LXX, the noun διακονία occurs only once in an apocryphal book (1 Maccabees 11:58), and the noun διάκονος appears only rarely: it is used to translate the piel participle of שׁרת 3 times (Esther 1:10, 2:2, 6:3) and the noun נַעַר once (Esther 6:5); it also occurs in places with no MT equivalent twice (4 Maccabees 9:17; addition to Proverbs 10:4).

10 Beyer, 'διακονέω, διακονία, διάκονος' (ET), p 82. The original is even more emphatic: 'ihm ursprünglich ein ganz bestimmter anshaulicher Sinn zugrunde liegt, der auch in den übertragenen Bedeutungen des Wortes noch nachklingt' (p 81).

11 Beyer, 'διακονέω, διακονία, διάκονος' (ET), p 87. Original: 'jede Dienstleistung, die aus rechter Liebesgesinnung heraus geschieht' (p 87).

12 Beyer, 'διακονέω, διακονία, διάκονος' (ET), p 87. Original: 'jede für den Aufbau wichtige Betätigung in der Gemeinde' (p 87).

13 Indeed, the welfare agency of the German Lutheran Churches, employing around half a million people, is named *Diakonisches Werk*: see John N Collins, 'Re-Interpreting *Diakonia* in Germany,' *Ecclesiology* 5 (2009), p 70.

14 Klaus Hess, 'Serve, Deacon, Worship,' ed. Colin Brown, *The New International Dictionary of New Testament Theology* (Exeter: Paternoster, 1978), p 546.

> Testament's choice of this word is all the more striking in that the basic meaning 'to serve at table' is still current throughout, as is the general meaning 'to serve'.[15]
>
> The very choice of the word, which still clearly involves the idea of humble activity, proves that the Church wishes to denote the attitude of one who is at the service of God and his fellow-men, not a position carrying with it rights and powers.[16]

On the passage that concerns us here, Ephesians 4:11-12, Markus Barth in his 1974 commentary writes:

> In summary, the task of the special ministers mentioned in Ephesians 4:11 is to be servants in that ministry which is entrusted to the whole church. Their place is not above but below the great number of saints who are not adorned by resounding titles. Every one of the special ministers is a *servus servorum Dei* ... In turn, the task of the whole church and of every saint is to carry out a work of service for the praise of God and the benefit of all who need it.[17]

Moving forward to 1990, Andrew Lincoln writes in his commentary on Ephesians 4:11-12:

> These officers are Christ's gifts to the Church, but again it becomes clear that such a perspective on their role should never lead to self-glorification. They have been given to carry out the work of service, and it is service which provides the framework for understanding any ministerial function or office[18]

The claim that διακονία means 'service' has also affected many of our translations, especially those closer to the 'dynamic equivalence' end of the translation spectrum. Modern translations of Ephesians 4:12a include: 'to prepare his people for works of service' (*NIV*), 'to prepare all God's people for the work of Christian service' (*GNT*) and 'to train Christ's followers in skilled servant work' (*The Message*).

1.2.3. *Challenged*

The question Collins forces us to ask is this: Is this interpretation of διακονία as 'service' in Ephesians 4:12 legitimate? Of course, it cannot

---

15 Eduard Schweizer, *Church Order in the New Testament*, SBT 32 (London: SCM, 1971), pp 174-175.

16 Schweizer, *Church Order*, p 177.

17 Barth, *Ephesians*, p 481.

18 Andrew T Lincoln, *Ephesians*, WBC 42 (Dallas: Word, 1990), p 254.

be denied that there are key places in the Gospels where Jesus uses the διακον- word-group in the context of 'waiting at tables' (e.g. Luke 12:37, 22:27) and he often draws out implications involving humble service (e.g. Mark 9:35). However, this observation by itself does not mean that 'waiting at tables' is the basic, 'original' sense which influences all other uses of the word. We need to guard against the problem diagnosed by James Barr (in reference to the *TDNT*), which he labelled 'illegitimate totality transfer'.[19] The problem occurs when we forget that 'any one instance of a word will not bear all the meanings possible for that word.'[20] Is, then, the claim that 'ministry' always means 'service' an instance of illegitimate totality transfer?

Dieter Georgi

An early challenge to the notion was mounted in 1964 by Dieter Georgi in his work on 2 Corinthians.[21] Georgi re-examined a number of the sources and contested the prevailing consensus that Paul's work as a 'minister' or διάκονος should be understood primarily in terms of humble service. Georgi conceded that sometimes the word means table-waiter, but often it means something quite different. For Georgi, the key background is that of a Cynic notion:

> The διακονία of the true Cynic therefore consists in being messenger, scout, the herald of the gods ... Thus the διακονία of the Cynic is the expression of his world-encompassing missionary consciousness. He sees himself as God's representative in the world; he has a mission in and to the entire world.[22]

---

19 James Barr, *The Semantics of Biblical Language* (Oxford: Oxford University Press, 1961), p 218.

20 Moisés Silva, *Biblical Words and Their Meaning: An Introduction to Lexical Semantics*, rev. and exp. ed. (Grand Rapids: Zondervan, 1994), p 25. See also Donald A Carson, *Exegetical Fallacies* (Grand Rapids: Baker, 1984), p 62: 'The fallacy in this instance lies in the supposition that the meaning of a word in a specific context is much broader than the context itself allows and may bring with it the word's entire semantic range'. Cf. Frederick W Danker, '*Diakonia*: Re-Interpreting the Ancient Sources by John N Collins / Die Diakonie der Gerechtigkeit und der Versöhnung in der Apologie des 2. Korintherbriefes: Analyse und Auslegung von 2 Kor 2,14-4,6; 5:11–6:10, by Anacleto de Oliviera,' *Crit. Rev. Books Relig.* (1991): p 181.

21 Dieter Georgi, *Die Gegner des Paulus im 2. Korintherbrief, Wissenschaftliche Monographien zum Alten und Neuen Testament 11* (Neukirchen-Vluyn, 1964). ET *The Opponents of Paul in Second Corinthians, Studies of the New Testament and Its World* (Edinburgh: T&T Clark, 1987), pp 27-32.

22 Georgi, *Opponents*, p 28.

For Georgi, this concept of 'missionary consciousness' is sufficient to understand the New Testament usage, including the usage in Ephesians 4:12. Thus:

> The NT term almost never involves an act of charity. Instead, nearly all instances are meant to refer to acts of proclamation.[23]

Georgi's observations were significant, but too brief, and did not allow for sufficient nuance or depth to provide a significant change in the understanding of the term.

John Collins

John Collins' work does, however, provide the necessary nuance and detailed re-examination of the sources needed for a thoroughgoing challenge. Collins notes that the idea of 'waiting at table' cannot be called the 'basic meaning' of the verb διακονέω. Admittedly, the concept of 'waiting at table' does appear in about a quarter of all instances in the sources, but this statistic alone is not sufficient – indeed, about half of these instances occur in a single work about dinner parties (Athenaeus's *Deipnosophistae*)![24]

Rather, Collins points to other, more pervasive underlying notions for the use of the word-group. The διάκονος, for example is very often some sort of 'go-between'. The word-group is often used to connote movement, or carrying something. In Plato's *Republic*, for example, the word διάκονος refers to a (hypothetical) free citizen with a task of being a 'trader', 'courier'. The word is not chosen in order to express the humility of the citizen's task; rather it simply refers to someone who carries something from one person or place to another.[25]

About a third of all instances of the διακον- word-group involve the conveying of messages – i.e. carrying a 'word' from one person to another.[26] Indeed, the word-group often has religious overtones, and is used in contexts where a message is brought from heaven to earth.[27] Two key passages in this regard are found in Josephus, *B.J.* 3.354, 4.626,

---

[23] Georgi, *Opponents*, p 29.

[24] Collins, *Diakonia*, 75. In any case, even in the places where the διακον- word-group is used to refer to table-waiting, the sense of a menial status or servility is not necessarily in the foreground. The use of the word draws attention to the type of 'fetching' activity involved in table-waiting, rather than to the status of the table-waiter (p 156).

[25] Collins, *Diakonia*, pp 78-79, 146.

[26] Collins, *Diakonia*, p 96.

[27] Collins, *Diakonia*, pp 96-132.

where Josephus uses the word διάκονος as a job description for himself. Josephus portrays himself as a bringer of a momentous message to the future Roman Emperor concerning God's will for the Empire and for the nations.[28] Here it is certainly not a word denoting humility; in fact, the Emperor Vespasian expresses how *unfitting* it is for a διάκονος to be found in humble circumstances:

> It is a shameful thing (said he) that this man who hath foretold my coming to the empire beforehand, and been the minister (διάκονος) of a divine message to me, should still be retained in the condition of a captive or prisoner. (Josephus, *B.J.* 4.626 [Whiston])

Here we see the term διάκονος used within a narrative 'charged with ideas of divine inspiration, election, and mission'.[29] This helps us to understand one of the key uses of the διακον- word-group for the Apostle Paul himself in the Corinthian letters: that is, the idea of being a 'spokesman' of God and/or a 'medium' of divine revelation and blessings (see esp. 1 Corinthians 3:5; 2 Corinthians 3:6, 6:4, 11:23).[30] Furthermore, it is close to the use of the term διάκονος in Ephesians 3:7 where Paul describes himself as a person dispensing heavenly knowledge:[31]

> Of this gospel I was made a minister (διάκονος) according to the gift of God's grace, which was given me by the working of his power. To me, though I am the very least of all the saints, this grace was given, to preach to the Gentiles the unsearchable riches of Christ, and to bring to light for everyone what is the plan of the mystery hidden for ages in God who created all things, ... (Ephesians 3:7-8)

For Paul in Ephesians, then, being a διάκονος means being a 'bringer' – in this instance, a 'bringer' of heavenly knowledge to the world. We will see in a moment that this has a bearing on the use of the term διακονία in Ephesians 4:12. Before examining this text, however, we will briefly survey how Collins' now 25-year-old thesis has been received by scholars.

1.2.4. *The Challenge Applauded*

Collins' thesis was warmly applauded by many in the English-speaking world when it was published. Karl Donfried, for example, writing soon after Collins' work was published, described it as 'magnificent' and 'meticulous'

---

[28] Collins, *Diakonia*, pp 111-115.

[29] Collins, *Diakonia*, p 115.

[30] Collins, *Diakonia*, pp 195-216.

[31] Collins, 'Re-Interpreting *Diakonia*,' p 233.

before going about applying Collins' insights to his own (American Lutheran) church life.[32] Paula Gooder, writing 16 years later, notes:

> Collins has never been criticized for his linguistic findings on the Hellenistic usage of the word group. Most scholars seem to accept that his findings and interpretation of the Hellenistic material are accurate.[33]

For Gooder, the value of Collins' research for New Testament scholarship is that it 'broadens the linguistic basis' for understanding the διακον- word-group.[34] It prevents us from jumping to the conclusion that the 'meaning' of the word-group must be 'menial service', and allows us to look at other possibilities.

It is most significant that Frederick Danker, the reviser of Bauer's standard Greek lexicon (*BDAG*), both gave Collins' work a glowing review,[35] and also used Collins' findings to thoroughly revise the relevant entries in his lexicon. Thus, although the second (1979) edition of the lexicon lists as the first meaning of each of the respective elements of the word-group: 'wait on someone at table', 'service' and 'servant',[36] the third (2000) edition of the lexicon has been revised: the first meaning of each of the respective elements of the word-group are now: 'to function as an intermediary', 'service rendered in an intermediary capacity' and 'one who serves as an intermediary in a transaction'.[37]

In the German-speaking world, Anni Hentschel has written a significant monograph on the meaning of the term διακονία. While her work is largely independent of Collins, she accepts Collins' basic approach to the ancient sources, and comes to conclusions that are similar to his, albeit not identical. Hentschel prefers to see in the

---

32 Karl P Donfried, 'Ministry: Rethinking the Term *Diakonia,*' *Concordia Theol.* Q. 56, no. 1 (1992), p 2.

33 Paula Gooder, '*Diakonia* in the New Testament: A Dialogue with John N. Collins,' *Ecclesiology* 3, no. 1 (2006), p 47.

34 Gooder, '*Diakonia,*' p 48.

35 Danker, '*Diakonia* / Die Diakonie,' pp 181-182.

36 Walter Bauer et al., *A Greek-English Lexicon of the New Testament and Other Early Christian Literature,* 2nd ed. (Chicago: University of Chicago Press, 1979), pp 184-185.

37 Walter Bauer et al., *A Greek-English Lexicon of the New Testament and Other Early Christian Literature,* 3rd ed. (Chicago: University of Chicago Press, 2000), pp 229-231.

διακον- word-group a fundamental notion of 'commission' or 'mandate'.[38] Collins has provided a detailed review and response.[39]

1.2.5. *The Challenge Overlooked*

There are few, if any, articles and commentaries that actively oppose the core of Collins' thesis. Nevertheless, in many cases, scholars are still unaware of his ground-breaking work.[40] This is certainly the case when it comes to commentaries on Ephesians. For example, the significant commentaries by O'Brien (1999) and Hoehner (2002) follow the older view that the word διακονία basically means 'service'.[41] These and other commentaries make statements such as: 'the work of ministry ... refers to the common service of all believers';[42] 'The noun διακονία ... conveys the idea of serving the Lord by ministering to one another';[43] 'the work of service depicts a disposition toward these gifts given by Christ ... best displayed in service rather than self-aggrandizement'.[44]

---

38 German '*Beauftragung*'. See Anni Hentschel, *Diakonia im Neuen Testament: Studien zur Semantik unter besonderer Berücksichtigung der Rolle von Frauen* (Tübingen: Mohr Siebeck, 2007). This is similar to Gooder's view: 'In my view the most significant and persuasive outcome of Collins's interpretation is that ministry is not primarily about caring for one's neighbours but about fulfilling a task commissioned by a master (whether this be in the case of a 'normal' servant or in the case of a servant of God or of the church).' (Gooder, '*Diakonia*,' p 54).

39 Collins, 'Re-Interpreting *Diakonia*.'

40 Gooder, '*Diakonia*,' p 46.

41 Peter T O'Brien, *The Letter to the Ephesians, The Pillar New Testament Commentary* (Grand Rapids: Eerdmans, 1999), p 303 n 127, as expected, refers to the earlier (pre-2000) version of Bauer's lexicon.

42 O'Brien, *Ephesians*, pp 303-304.

43 Harold W Hoehner, *Ephesians: An Exegetical Commentary* (Grand Rapids: Baker Academic, 2002), p 550.

44 Stephen E Fowl, *Ephesians: A Commentary, The New Testament Library* (Louisville, Kentucky: Westminster John Knox, 2012), p 142. See also Clinton E Arnold, *Ephesians, Zondervan Exegetical Commentary on the New Testament* (Grand Rapids: Zondervan, 2010), pp 262-263; William J Larkin, *Ephesians: A Handbook on the Greek Text, Baylor Handbook on the Greek New Testament* (Waco, Texas: Baylor University Press, 2009), p 79. Ernest Best, *Ephesians* (London: T & T Clark International, 1998), p 396, refers to Collins but seems to have given the book too cursory a reading; he wrongly takes the term διακονία to mean simply 'communication', which he then subsumes under the category of 'service'. More surprisingly, a 2001 article in the *Expository Times* expressly addressing the issue of what the word διακονία means in Ephesians 4:12 makes no reference to Collins' work: J C O'Neill, '"The Work of the Ministry" in Ephesians 4:12 and the New Testament,' *Expository Times* 112 (2001), pp 336-40. Interestingly, O'Neill's argument would have been greatly strengthened had Collins' work come to his attention before he wrote his article. O'Neill laments the rise of a view that sees church ministers simply as managers, organisers and motivators of the 'real' ministry

1.2.6. *The Challenge Critiqued / Modified*

Other scholars have taken Collins' insights on board, while modifying or critiquing individual aspects of his thesis. Collins has been critiqued by some who claim he places too much weight on the concept of the 'messenger',[45] and by others for his relative lack of emphasis on concepts of humility and service *associated* with ministry.[46] This lack of emphasis is understandable given Collins' particular interest in recovering the dignity of clerical calling.[47] He tends to concentrate on the Pauline references, and his emphasis falls on the exalted nature of the office of the διάκονος as a bearer of God's word to people. This can leave the impression that Collins is uninterested in instances where the word-group is clearly *associated* with humble service – not only in Jesus' words in the Gospels (e.g. Luke 17:7-10, Luke 22:24-27), but also in Paul's letters (e.g. 1 Corinthians 3:5-7).

It is important to note, however, that Collins himself is *not* claiming that ancient or modern ideas of ministry have no place at all for 'humble service'. He is simply claiming that 'ministry' and 'humble service' are not synonyms. For Collins, the most pervasive element of the διακον- word-group is that of the 'go-between'. In many instances we could render this as 'bringer': the word-group may denote activities as varied as bringing dishes to a table and bringing a message from the gods to humanity. It can also be used more broadly to refer to tasks or offices involving attendance or assistance. Thus, while any given instance of the

---

which is done by lay people. O'Neill accepts that 'minister' means 'servant', but attempts to work against the more radical implications of this observation by arguing that a 'servant' of people is also a 'servant' of God and therefore also has authority.

[45] 'According to Collins, the principle [sic] meaning of the concept is connected to the role of messenger': Latvus, 'The Paradigm Challenged,' pp 144, 149. This is a little unfair to Collins, who in fact sees the concept of the 'go-between' as broader than the concept of the 'messenger'.

[46] I am grateful to the insights of Colin Marshall, 'What Is "Ministry" and Who Are the "Ministers"? An Evaluation of John Collins' Re-Interpretation of *Diakonia* in the New Testament and Implications for Contemporary Views of the Diaconate and Lay Ministry.' (Unpublished MA Project, Moore Theological College, 2007), pp 16-24.

[47] E.g. Collins, *Diakonia*, pp 20-41.

διακον- word-group may certainly *connote* 'humble service' (e.g. Mark 9:35, 43, 45),[48] it does not in every instance *mean* 'humble service'.[49]

1.3. *Who does the 'Work of Ministry' in Ephesians 4:11-12?*

In Ephesians, as we have seen, the concept of the 'go-between' takes on a distinct form. In Ephesians 3:7, Paul describes himself as being a 'bringer' (διάκονος) of heavenly knowledge to the world, with some parallels to Josephus' description of himself as a 'bringer' (διάκονος) of a divine message to the Emperor (*B.J.* 3.354, 4.626). The most natural meaning of the term 'ministry' (διακονία) in Ephesians 4:12, therefore, is the activity of 'bringing' God's word to the world, thus mediating divine revelation and blessing.[50]

We now turn to look more closely at the significance of the term in Ephesians 4:11-12. The first question that interpreters often ask when approaching these verses is this: Who actually performs the work of ministry?[51] Do the officials of verse 11 perform the work of ministry, or do the saints of verse 12 perform the work of ministry? Verse 12 can be punctuated in two different ways, leading to two different answers. It all depends on where one places the comma!

1.3.1. *The 'officials' (esp. the Pastors / Teachers) do the 'Work of Ministry'?*

Translations before the mid-20th century generally placed a comma after the word 'saints' in verse 12.[52] This punctuation implies that verse 12 consists of three co-ordinate prepositional phrases, all describing the activity of the officials in verse 11. In this understanding, Ephesians 4:11-12 reads:

---

48 Collins, *Diakonia*, p 252, understands Mark 10:45 as follows: 'the Son of man is not one who holds such a position in the world as to have attendants – the διάκονοι of the rich and powerful – coming up to him and being despatched by him about the various tasks of his own choosing; he has his own task to go to, and it is for the purpose of setting the profane grandeur of one way of life against the prophetic dedication of the other that Mark has brought these oddly fitting infinitives together.'

49 Cf. Gooder, '*Diakonia*,' p 55.

50 Collins, *Diakonia*, p 233.

51 T David Gordon, '"Equipping" Ministry in Ephesians 4?,' *J. Evang. Theol. Soc.* 37, no. 1 (1994), p 69.

52 This understanding is reflected in the *KJV*, *RV* and the first edition of the *RSV*. See also John Calvin, *Institutes of the Christian Religion*, ed. John T McNeill, trans. Ford Lewis Battles, 2 vols. (Louisville, Kentucky: Westminster John Knox, 1960), § 4.3.2, p 1055.

> And [Christ] gave the apostles, the prophets, the evangelists, and the pastors and teachers,
> [1.] for the equipping of the saints,
> [2.] for [the] work of ministry,
> [3.] for [the] building of the body of Christ

In this understanding, the work of ministry is done by the 'officials' of verse 11 – or by the 'officials' mentioned last, i.e. the pastors / teachers. 'The saints' do not do the work of ministry, they simply receive it. This is Collins' view, which he finds consistent with his argument that διακονία must involve dispensing heavenly knowledge:

> The author of Ephesians also celebrates gifts in the church but is speaking only of gifts upon teachers ('pastors' being taken as part of these; Ephesians 4:11). This is in accord with the emphasis that the epistle has earlier placed on the communication of God's mystery, the process where Paul had the leading role as διάκονος (3:7); the emphasis on teaching is also in accord with the outcomes held up for emulation in this passage, namely, unity in faith, solidarity in doctrine, and maturity in truth (4:13-16). With teaching then the overriding theme and teachers the only figures mentioned, the 'work of ministry' (ἔργον διακονίας, 4:12) can only be understood as part of this teaching process within the church so that it signifies here, against the background of the heavenly Christ dispensing his word through teachers, the work done by the kind of 'minister' who dispenses heavenly knowledge (Ephesians 3:7; Colossians 1:7, 23, 25); the usage is close in meaning to instances at 2 Corinthians 3:7-9; 5:18.[53]

This view is not Collins' alone; it has enjoyed something of a 'revival' among a number of other modern authors, many of whom, like Collins, are seeking to uphold the significance of the distinct teaching offices.[54]

In its favour, this view is consistent with the most likely semantic field of διακονία in Ephesians, i.e. the idea of bringing God's revelation to people. Just as Paul can describe his own apostolic role as that of a διάκονος (Ephesians 3:7), so too the teachers of the church can be described in terms of διακονία, i.e. dispensing God's word.

---

53 Collins, *Diakonia*, p 233.

54 Gordon, '"Equipping" Ministry'; Henry P Hamaan, 'The Translation of Ephesians 4:12: A Necessary Revision,' *Concordia* J. 14, no. 1 (1988), pp 42-49; Lincoln, *Ephesians*, pp 253-254; Marshall, 'What Is "Ministry",' pp 25-29; O'Neill, 'The Work of the Ministry.'

However, this view is not without its problems, which we can see more clearly when we examine the alternative view.

1.3.2. *The 'Work of Ministry' is for 'The Saints'?*

A second understanding of the passage, reflected in most modern translations (e.g. the *ESV*), removes the comma after the word 'saints'. In this understanding, Ephesians 4:11-12 reads:

> And [Christ] gave the apostles, the prophets, the evangelists, and the pastors and teachers,
> --> for the equipping of the saints
> --> for [the] work of ministry
> --> for [the] building of the body of Christ

In this view, 'the work of ministry' is an activity for 'the saints' (usually understood as the whole church); and the task of the officials in verse 11 is to equip the saints for their work of ministry.

This view was put forward forcefully by Markus Barth, in his 1974 commentary on Ephesians, in a stridently anti-clerical section titled 'The Church without Laymen and Priests'.[55] Barth believes that the former interpretation has an:

> aristocratic, that is, a clerical and ecclesiastic flavour; it distinguishes the (mass of the) 'saints' from the (superior class of the) officers of the church. A clergy is now distinct from the laity, to whom the privilege and burden of carrying out the prescribed construction work are exclusively assigned.[56]

By contrast, Barth argues, removing the comma means that:

> All the saints (and among them, each saint) are enabled by the four or five types of servants enumerated in 4:11 to fulfil the ministry given to them, so that the whole church is taken into Christ's service and given missionary substance, purpose and structure.[57]

Before we dismiss this view as being too driven by the democratic, anti-clerical, 'every member ministry' mindset of the mid-to-late 20th

[55] Barth, *Ephesians*, pp 477-484.
[56] Barth, *Ephesians*, p 479.
[57] Barth, *Ephesians*, p 479.

century, we need to realise that there are at least two significant exegetical arguments in its favour.[58]

Firstly, the Greek construction used for the first phrase is different to the construction used for the second and third phrases. The first phrase, 'for the equipping of the saints' uses the preposition πρός + the article. The second two phrases, 'for [the] work of ministry' and 'for [the] building of the body of Christ', use a different preposition (εἰς) and no article. While the change in prepositions is not decisive in itself, when combined with the lack of article there is a reasonably strong argument that the 'saints' are the ones who do the 'work of ministry'.[59]

Secondly, 'the saints' are mentioned at the end of the first phrase. This suggests that there is a shift in focus at that point from the prior group (the officials of verse 11), to a new group, 'the saints'.[60] Again, this implies that it is the 'saints' who do the 'work of ministry.'[61]

However, despite these exegetical arguments in favour of this view, the glaring problem remains: it does not seem to fit with the conclusion we came to above, that the word 'ministry' (διακονία) in this particular context (i.e. in Ephesians) is best understood as referring to a specific activity in 'bringing' a message or revelation from God to people (cf. Paul's special role as διάκονος in Ephesians 3:7). The meaning of the word in this context seems to fit more comfortably with the particular 'offices' of verse 11 than it does with something that the whole church does. Hentschel tentatively suggests that the word διακονία functions in a special way here: it elevates regular Christian word and deed to the level of a 'commission' from God to build Christ's body.[62] However, again, this solution is an extra level of abstraction that does not fit easily with any of the known uses of the word.

---

58 I am grateful to my colleague Peter Orr for his insights on this matter, in Peter Orr, 'Paul as Pastor in Ephesians' (paper presented at the Paul as Pastor conference, Ridley College, Melbourne, 2014).

59 Frank Thielman, *Ephesians*, Baker Exegetical Commentary on the New Testament (Grand Rapids: Baker, 2010), p 278. O'Neill, 'The Work of the Ministry,' p 339, points to some miniscules that omit the article, but the evidence is not strong.

60 O'Brien, *Ephesians*, pp 302-303.

61 A third argument involves the fact that the 'work of ministry' is equivalent to 'building the body' (verse 12), which a few verses later is described as a task for the whole body (verse 16): See e.g. Hentschel, *Diakonia*, pp 393-394; Craig Loscalzo, 'Ephesians 4:1-16,' *Rev. Expo.* 85 (1988), pp 687-91. See also the rhetorical analysis by Juan Manuel Granados Rojas, 'Ephesians 4,12: A Revised Reading,' *Biblica* 92, no. 1 (2011), pp 81-96. This argument assumes, however, that 'the saints' means 'the whole body', an assumption that we will question below.

62 Hentschel, *Diakonia*, pp 393-395.

Thus we seem to be at an impasse. If we cannot answer the question of 'Who does the work of ministry?', how will we be able to understand what the work of ministry is?

We will now offer an important corrective, followed by a proposed solution.

1.4. *The movement from truth to unity in Ephesians 4:7-16*

The discussion of Ephesians 4:11-12 is often dominated by pragmatic questions concerning church order, structure and roles. These present-day questions, however, are not necessarily the concern of this passage. In fact, there is good reason to conclude that Paul is not here describing a static model of church order, but rather is portraying a stage in the *temporal* movement of gospel truth from the ascended Christ, through the agency of certain gifts, to 'the whole body'.

In Ephesians 4:1-6, Paul exhorts the Ephesian Christians to maintain the 'unity' to which they have been 'called' – a loving unity based on the truth of the gospel (cf. Ephesians 1:13, 17-18).[63] In verses 7-16, Paul describes how this truth-based unity is achieved in God's plan. The unity comes about through a dynamic process – a process that begins with a diversity of gifts (verse 7) and ends with a united body (verse 16). There are three features to notice about this process. Firstly, it involves a movement of *God's word* from Christ to his people. Secondly, it involves a *temporal* movement from past to future. Thirdly, it begins with special individuals, and ends with 'all' members of the body.

Firstly, the process involves a movement of *God's word* from Christ to his people. The initial 'gifts' of the ascended Christ are people with 'speaking' offices (verse 11), and the result is that all members of Christ's body are 'speaking the truth [of the gospel] in love' together (verses 15-16).[64]

---

[63] Barth, *Ephesians*, p 480; Loscalzo, 'Ephesians 4:1-16,' p 688.

[64] For a strong argument that the verb ἀληθεύω here refers to 'speaking the truth' rather than simply 'living out the truth' see O'Brien, *Ephesians*, pp 310-311. The verb means 'speaking the truth' consistently in the LXX (Genesis 20:16; 42:16; Proverbs 21:3; Isaiah 44:26; Sirach 34:4); elsewhere in Galatians it refers to speaking the truth of the gospel (Galatians 4:16, cf. 2:5, 14). The 'truth' in Ephesians 1:13 is the truth of the gospel.

Secondly, the process involves a *temporal* movement from past to future. Certain events have already occurred in the past. Christ descended, ascended and gave gifts to his people (verses 8-10). Some of these gifts consisted of certain special 'offices' (verse 11), which lead to the 'equipping of the saints for the work of ministry, for the building of the body of Christ' (verse 12). In verse 13, Paul turns to describe a projected future result: a time when 'we all attain to the unity of faith' (verse 13), no longer shaken by every false teaching (verse 14), but all participating in a self-growing body (verse 16). Verses 13-16 are future-oriented: the verses are dominated by three subjunctive verbs, with adverbs indicating future time and a conjunction indicating purpose or result: 'until we arrive' (μέχρι καταντήσωμεν, verse 13),[65] 'so that we may no longer be' (ἵνα μηκέτι ὦμεν, verse 14), and '[so that] we may grow up' ([ἵνα] ... αὐξήσωμεν, verse 15). This implies that Paul in verses 13-16 is envisaging a future state.

Thirdly, the process described in verses 11-16 begins with special individuals, and ends with 'all' members of the body. Verse 11 describes the particular 'gifts' of Christ: apostles, prophets, evangelists, pastors and teachers. In verse 13, however, as soon as the future comes into view, the emphasis is on 'all' members of the body. The future state involves 'all of us' (οἱ πάντες + first person plural verb) attaining to 'unity' (verse 13). The terms 'all' (πᾶς), 'one' (εἷς), and 'we' (i.e. first person plural verbs) continue to recur throughout verses 13-16. Thus verses 13-16 are marked out from what precedes them not only by their future orientation, but also by their focus on 'all' members of the body as opposed to the earlier focus on the particular 'gifts'.

What future state is Paul envisaging? Commentators often state that verse 13 is describing an ideal and / or post-parousia eschatological state to which the church will never actually attain in this age but towards which it should constantly strive.[66] However, this is at odds with the flow of the passage. The verses that immediately follow verse 13 (verses 14-16) are clearly not describing a final eschatological state; rather they are describing the truth-and-love-based 'growth' of the

---

65 Hoehner, *Ephesians*, p 552; O'Brien, *Ephesians*, p 305.

66 Barth, *Ephesians*, pp 484-496; Best, *Ephesians*, p 403; Hoehner, *Ephesians*, p 558; Lincoln, *Ephesians*, pp 256-257; O'Brien, *Ephesians*, pp 305-308; Thielman, *Ephesians*, pp 282-283. O'Brien explains this in terms of the 'eschatological tension between the already and the not yet' (p 306); Hoehner explains it as something that is 'possible for this age but may not be completed until the future, possibly when the church meets her Lord' (p 558).

earthly body of Christ. Rather than assuming that Paul jumps from the past or present (verses 11-12) to the future (verse 13) and back to the present (verses 14-16), it is worth considering the possibility that the entirety of verses 13-16 is speaking of the same future-yet-pre-parousia state of affairs.[67] This possibility is greatly strengthened when we observe Paul's choice of the term 'unity' (ἑνότης) to describe the future state in verse 13. This word does not refer back to the final, eschatological 'summing up of all things' in Christ (cf. 1:10) but rather refers back to the 'unity of the Spirit' (4:3) which is effective in Christian lives before the eschaton (cf. 1:13-14). It also recalls the unity of Jew and Gentile in 'one' (εἷς) new humanity and one body (2:14-16).

It seems, then, that Paul is looking forward to a time in the future in which the 'unity of the Spirit' will be realised in a greater way than it was at his time. This will occur because the 'truth' of the gospel will be permeating 'all' members of the body rather than just some, which means that the body will be able to build *itself* up rather than constantly being shaken by false teaching. This unity may well be caught up with the unity of Jew and Gentile described in 2:14-16. It will be the end-point of a process that involves a movement of God's word from Christ, through special individuals, to 'all' members of the body.

How does this affect our understanding of the 'work of ministry' in verse 12? It helps us to see that the 'work of ministry' is part of a movement of God's word from Christ to his body. Just as Paul's special apostolic role as the διάκονος bringing God's revelation to the Gentiles (3:7) was a particular stage in God's plan (the οἰκονομία, 3:2), so the 'work of διακονία' in Ephesians 4:12 is also describing a stage in God's plan – it is not the whole of the plan, nor the end goal of the plan. It is also possible that the future state envisaged by Paul (i.e. the *whole* body speaking the truth in love to one another) has already occurred in our time, which would mean that the particular 'work of ministry' described in Ephesians 4:12 has been fulfilled – just as Paul's particular role as διάκονος has also been fulfilled.

---

67 This is true whether we regard verses 14-16 as parallel to verse 13 (Arnold, *Ephesians*, p 267; Fowl, *Ephesians*, p 143; Hoehner, *Ephesians*, p 560; Lincoln, *Ephesians*, p 257) or as describing the purpose / result of verse 13 (O'Brien, *Ephesians*, p 308).

1.5. *A proposed solution: 'The saints' as Jewish Christians?*

So then: What *is* the work of ministry? Let us assume for the moment that the exegetical arguments outlined above are in favour of 'the saints' as the ones who do the 'work of ministry'. Now, let us ask the further question: Who *are* 'the saints?'

It is normally assumed that 'the saints' are all Christians, i.e. that the term is intended to refer to all of Paul's addressees, and that they are the equivalent of the 'whole body' (Ephesians 4:16). However, Donald Robinson, former lecturer in New Testament at Moore College, has questioned this assumption.[68] Robinson looked at other instances of the term 'the saints' in Paul's letters, especially in Colossians and Ephesians. Although of course the Gentile addressees of Ephesians are called 'holy' (ἅγιος) by virtue of their relationship with Christ (e.g. Ephesians 2:21, 5:27), in certain places in Ephesians and Colossians the phrase '*the* saints' (οἱ ἅγιοι, with the article) seems to refer to a group distinct from the addressees, a group whose holy status and blessings flow *to* the addressees. So for example, Ephesians 2:19 reads:

> So then you are no longer strangers and aliens, but you are fellow citizens **with the saints** (τῶν ἁγίων) and members of the household of God (Ephesians 2:19).

Robinson suggested that the phrase 'the saints' most naturally refers to the very early *Jewish* Christians (cf. Ephesians 2:11-12), i.e. those with the original 'inheritance', in which the Gentile Christians have become qualified to share (Ephesians 1:18, 3:18). On Ephesians 4:12, then, Robinson writes:

> Are 'the saints' in this passage all believers? This is possible, but we are not shut up to such an interpretation. Referred to the ministry of Jewish believers, it [i.e. 'the work of ministering'] makes excellent sense. It was through the work of the apostles and prophets (cf. 2:20; 3:5), the evangelists, pastors and teachers, that the primitive Jewish body of believers was fitted and prepared to fulfil its foreordained role of being the Lord's 'minister' (διάκονος) or servant to the nations, and so 'build the body of Christ' which was the new unity of Jew and Gentile. To take 'ministering' with reference to preaching the gospel to the Gentiles is in line with Paul's application of this term διάκονος to himself in 3:7 and probably rests

---

68 Donald W B Robinson, 'Who Were "the Saints"?,' *Reform. Theol. Rev.* 22, no. 2 (1963), pp 45-53.

> on passages like Isaiah 49:6 where the task of the 'servant' is not merely the restoration of Israel but the bringing of salvation to the Gentiles (cf. Acts 15:16f.).[69]

Robinson, then, understands the 'work of ministry' as the corporate responsibility of the early Jewish Christians to bring the gospel of Christ to the nations. Of course, because Robinson was writing in the mid-twentieth century, he was assuming the pervasive notion that διακονία meant 'humble service'. This is why Robinson saw the need to connect the term διακονία with the Suffering Servant of Isaiah 49:6. Unfortunately, this connection is a little tenuous, since the word for 'Servant' in the LXX is δοῦλος not διάκονος.[70] However, if we also take into account Collins' insights about the semantic range of διακονία, the strained element of Robinson's exposition is removed.[71] The word can quite naturally refer to the task of 'bringing' – in this case, the early Jewish Christians collectively bringing the gospel of Christ to the nations (as in the cognate noun in 3:7, and cf. Josephus above).

May we then see 'the saints' as the renewed Israel, with the task to 'bring' God's revelation to the world (cf. e.g. Isaiah 2:2-5)? In Ephesians 3, Paul connects the term 'the saints' with his own special calling and ministry to preach Christ to the nations. Paul describes himself firstly as διάκονος, then 'least of all the saints,' and then preacher of Christ to the nations (Ephesians 3:7-8).[72] Given this connection that has already been established in Ephesians 3, it is natural

---

69 Robinson, 'Who Were "the Saints"?,' p 53.

70 Lionel Windsor, *Paul and the Vocation of Israel: How Paul's Jewish Identity Informs His Apostolic Ministry, with Special Reference to Romans*, BZNW 205 (Berlin: De Gruyter, 2014), pp 105-106.

71 Interestingly, 35 years later, after Robinson had interacted with Collins' insights and then returned to Ephesians 4:12, he favoured the traditional interpretation which regards the 'work of ministry' as a task for the officials alone:
'"For the work of ministry" could indeed indicate a purpose for which the saints had been 'perfected' or 'restored', but this is not required by the noun καταρισμός, and the traditional interpretation which takes 'for the work of διακονία' as part of Christ's purpose in giving the apostles, prophets, evangelists and pastor-teachers – indeed, as indicating their function – is more consonant with the thrust of the whole passage.
We conclude that διακονία in Ephesians 4:12 is still confined to the supreme ministry of the word exercised by those especially called and appointed by Christ.': Donald W B Robinson, 'Ministry/service in the Bible: Human and Divine, Secular and Sacred,' in *Forward in Faith? Proceedings of the 1996 Conference of the Association for the Apostolic Ministry* (Australia) (Enmore: Aquila Books (Australia), 1998), p 64.

72 Cf. 1 Corinthians 15:9, where Paul calls himself the 'least of the apostles' (Hentschel, *Diakonia*, p 394).

in Ephesians 4 to see Paul linking his own gospel-preaching ministry as διάκονος with a more general διακονία of the 'the saints', understood as the renewed Israel.

In this understanding of Ephesians 4:11-12, Paul is describing the situation of the very early church, consisting of Jewish believers, who were the first to hope in Christ (Ephesians 1:12). The ascended Christ gave them apostles, prophets, evangelists, pastor-teachers, who brought the gospel to them and so completed them for the 'work of ministry'. Through their knowledge of God's word in the Scriptures, completed in the gospel, they fulfilled their role as a holy people, the 'saints' – which meant collectively bringing God's revelation to the world. Ephesians 3 describes Paul, the least of all the saints, who is a particular minister (Ephesians 3). Ephesians 4 broadens this concept to a 'ministry' that belongs to the saints more generally, a ministry that involves 'bringing' the heavenly gospel of Christ to the nations. Paul looks forward to the time when this will lead, ultimately, to a united body, where all members, both Jewish and Gentile, share the truth of the gospel in love together (Ephesians 4:15-16).

This interpretation of Ephesians 4:11-16 should not be too surprising. We are simply suggesting that this passage is following the same pattern evident elsewhere in significant sections of Paul's letter to the Ephesians: a pattern that involves the historical movement of God's blessings / word from Israel to the nations. This pattern occurs in the introduction (1:11-14),[73] in the theologically central description of reconciliation (2:11-22), and in Paul's description of his own ministry (3:1, 6, 8). Thus it is likely that the pattern occurs here in 4:11-16 also.

On this understanding, a paraphrase of Ephesians 4:12 would read:

> to prepare the saints [i.e. God's particular people Israel] for the work of ministry [i.e. 'bringing' the revelation of Christ to the nations] for the building of Christ's body ...

1.6. *Implications*

If Ephesians 4:11-12 is describing a particular stage in the plan of God – i.e. if 'the saints' who do the 'work of ministry' are the early Jewish Christians through whom God brought the gospel of Christ to the world – we might ask how the passage could possibly apply to us today? This

---

73 O'Brien, *Ephesians*, pp 115-123.

is not as significant a problem as we might think. The same issue faces us as we seek to understand and apply Paul's role as διάκονος in Ephesians 3:1-13. Indeed, most of the Bible – from the Old Testament through the gospels through Acts – does not apply directly to us, but needs to be understood in its particular context in God's plan for salvation before being applied to us. This is just a regular task of biblical theology.

Where, then, do we fit into the plan of God outlined in this passage?

Most obviously and directly, we fit in to the situation of Ephesians 4:15-16. We are now living in the time when the gospel has been brought by the first Jewish believers to the nations. Our task as Christ's body is to benefit from that foundational 'work of ministry', which for us means to 'speak the truth in love' together and so to grow up into Christ, our head. The rest of Paul's letter to the Ephesians (4:17–6:20) spells out the practical implications of this in some detail, discussing issues of speech, truth, love, and diverse roles under the one Lord.

However, we might ask whether there is any special 'office' today that can be said to be charged with this particular 'work of ministry'. We cannot answer this question from Ephesians 4 alone. However, the Pastoral Epistles provide valuable insights for us. A number of times in the Pastoral Epistles, Paul uses the terms διακονία and διάκονος in a similar sense to his usage in Ephesians 3:7 and 4:11, to describe his and Timothy's roles as 'bringers' of divine revelation to the churches. The apostle himself has been specially appointed for 'ministry' (1 Timothy 1:12). Timothy also has a role as a 'minister' / 'ministry' (1 Timothy 4:6; 2 Timothy 4:5) – which involves opposing false teaching, promoting truth and love, and doing the work of an 'evangelist' (1 Timothy 1:3-7, 4:6-10; cf. 2 Timothy 4:1-5).[74] The doctrine of Christ that the 'ministers' bring to the communities must subsequently be passed on to various people who also have a role that involves opposing false teaching and promoting truth and right living, especially certain 'elders' (1 Timothy 5:17, Titus 1:5-9, cf. 2 Timothy 2:2).

There is a sense, then, in which church leaders / elders today have a role in continuing and extending the 'work of ministry' which was given to the apostles and the early church. As the whole body 'speaks the truth in love' together and thereby builds itself, there will be some individuals whose role it is to lead and guide us in that task, guarding the truth of

[74] Interestingly, Timothy is a Jewish believer (2 Timothy 3:15)

the gospel, refuting error, modelling and exhorting God's people to live and love in light of that truth. We could even call these people 'ministers' in a derivative sense, even if it would be going too far to label them διάκονοι in exactly the same exalted sense as we find it in, say, Ephesians 3:7.[75]

Notice, too, a further important implication arising from our investigation – an implication that applies regardless of what we decide about who 'the saints' are. If we see that the 'work of ministry' in Ephesians 4:12 means the 'task of bringing' – in this context, the task of bringing God's revelation to people – and does not *primarily* mean 'works of humble service', then God's word gains far more prominence. In the first instance, we can see that God's word is central to all of the activities in Ephesians 4:11-16. Ephesians 4:11-16 is *not* saying that there are certain special 'word ministers' (verse 11) whose job it is to equip other people for more varied non-word 'works of service' (verse 12 *NIV*). Rather, in Ephesians 4, it's God's word 'all the way down' – from Christ through the apostles, prophets, evangelists, pastors and teachers, through 'the saints' to the body whose job it is to 'speak the truth in love'.[76] This centrality of God's word, of course, also applies to the derivative 'ministry' and 'ministers' described in the pastoral epistles, and is applicable to us today.

What, then, of the problem we raised at the start of this essay? That is, if we conclude that 'ministry' does not necessarily mean 'loving, humble service' in Ephesians, have we removed the grounds to oppose clerical pride or ministry professionalization or the phenomenon of the celebrity pastor / preacher? Not at all: all we have lost is a slogan. We have other perfectly suitable words to promote the idea of 'humble service'. In Ephesians 4, the obvious examples are the words 'humility' (ταπεινοφροσύνη, Ephesians 4:2), and 'love' (ἀγάπη, Ephesians 4:2, 15-16). Even more importantly, we can and must constantly return to the truth that we have been saved by grace, so that we cannot boast (Ephesians 2:1-10). These concepts apply to all Christians, and therefore of course to pastors. Not only is it God's word 'all the way down,' it's also humility and love, 'all the way down' – for all those in Christ,

---

75 Nobody other than Paul or Timothy in the pastorals is designated as a 'minister' in the same sense that we find in Ephesians 3:7. The 'deacons' of 1 Timothy 3:8, 10, 12 are most likely 'assistants' to overseers rather than bearers of divine revelation (Collins, *Diakonia*, pp 237-238).

76 Despite his stridently 'anti-clerical' polemic, this is also Barth's view: he describes 'servants who act primarily by speaking' (Barth, *Ephesians*, p 483, cf. pp 479-480).

including the offices, the saints, and the body (4:2, 15). Any ministry performed in the name of Christ must always entail humility and love.

Nevertheless, the key point remains: 'ministry' does not *mean* 'humble service'. Whether it is apostles, saints, Israelites, pastors, teachers, elders or anyone else: the work of 'ministry' in Ephesians 4:12 always was, and still is, fundamentally a matter of 'bringing' – bringing the saving gospel of the Lord Jesus Christ to people.

1.7. *Bibliography*

Anglican Church Diocese of Sydney Department of Ministry Training & Development, *Full-Time Paid Ministry in the Diocese of Sydney* (2nd Edition) (Anglican Church Diocese of Sydney Department of Ministry Training & Development, 2009)

C E Arnold, *Ephesians*, Zondervan Exegetical Commentary on the New Testament (Grand Rapids: Zondervan, 2010)

J Barr, *The Semantics of Biblical Language* (Oxford: Oxford University Press, 1961)

M Barth, *Ephesians*. 2 vols, The Anchor Bible 34, 34A (Garden City: Doubleday, 1974)

W Bauer, W F Arndt, F W Gingrich, F W Danker, *A Greek-English Lexicon of the New Testament and Other Early Christian Literature*, 2nd ed. (Chicago: University of Chicago Press, 1979)

———, *A Greek-English Lexicon of the New Testament and Other Early Christian Literature*, 3rd ed. (Chicago: University of Chicago Press, 2000)

E Best, *Ephesians* (London: T & T Clark International, 1998)

H W Beyer, 'διακονέω, διακονία, διάκονος,' in *Theologisches Wörterbuch Zum Neuen Testament*, edited by G Kittel (Stuttgart: Kohlhammer, 1935)

———, 'διακονέω, διακονία, διάκονος,' in *Theological Dictionary of the New Testament*, edited by G Kittel, translated by G W Bromiley (Grand Rapids: Eerdmans, 1964)

J Calvin, *Institutes of the Christian Religion*, edited by John T. McNeill, translated by Ford Lewis Battles, 2 vols. (Louisville, Kentucky: Westminster John Knox, 1960)

D A Carson, *Exegetical Fallacies* (Grand Rapids: Baker, 1984)

J N Collins, *Diakonia: Re-Interpreting the Ancient Sources* (Oxford: Oxford University Press, 1990)

———, 'Re-Interpreting Diakonia in Germany,' *Ecclesiology* 5 (2009), pp 69-81

F W Danker, '*Diakonia*: Re-Interpreting the Ancient Sources by John N. Collins / Die Diakonie der Gerechtigkeit und der Versöhnung in der Apologie des 2 Korintherbriefes: Analyse und Auslegung von 2 Kor 2,14-4,6; 5:11-6:10, by Anacleto de Oliviera,' *Crit. Rev. Books Relig.* (1991), pp 181-84

K P Donfried, 'Ministry: Rethinking the Term Diakonia,' *Concordia Theol. Q.* 56, no. 1 (1992), pp 1-15.

R H Evans, 'When Jesus Meets TMZ: Why Celebrity Culture Is Overtaking Our Pulpits,' *Relevant* Magazine, 9 Feb 2012, http://www.relevantmagazine.com /god/church/features/28236-when-jesus-meets-tmz

S E Fowl, *Ephesians: A Commentary*, The New Testament Library (Louisville, Kentucky: Westminster John Knox, 2012)

D Georgi, *Die Gegner des Paulus im 2. Korintherbrief*, Wissenschaftliche Monographien zum Alten und Neuen Testament 11 (Neukirchen-Vluyn, 1964)

———, *The Opponents of Paul in Second Corinthians*, Studies of the New Testament and Its World (Edinburgh: T&T Clark, 1987)

P Gooder, '*Diakonia* in the New Testament: A Dialogue with John N. Collins,' *Ecclesiology* 3, no. 1 (2006), pp 33-56

T D Gordon, '"Equipping" Ministry in Ephesians 4?,' *J. Evang. Theol. Soc.* 37, no. 1 (1994), pp 69-78

J M Granados Rojas, 'Ephesians 4,12: A Revised Reading,' *Biblica* 92, no. 1 (2011), pp 81-96.

H P Hamaan, 'The Translation of Ephesians 4:12: A Necessary Revision,' *Concordia J.* 14, no. 1 (1988), pp 42-49

A Hentschel, Diakonia im Neuen Testament: Studien zur Semantik unter besonderer Berücksichtigung der Rolle von Frauen (Tübingen: Mohr Siebeck, 2007)

K Hess, 'Serve, Deacon, Worship,' pp 544-553 in *The New International Dictionary of New Testament Theology*, edited by Colin Brown (Exeter: Paternoster, 1978)

H W Hoehner, *Ephesians: An Exegetical Commentary* (Grand Rapids: Baker Academic, 2002)

W J Larkin, *Ephesians: A Handbook on the Greek Text*, Baylor Handbook on the Greek New Testament (Waco, Texas: Baylor University Press, 2009)

K Latvus, 'The Paradigm Challenged: A New Analysis of the Origin of *Diakonia*,' *Stud. Theol.* 62, no. 2 (2008), pp 142-57

A T Lincoln, *Ephesians*, Word Biblical Commentary 42 (Dallas: Word, 1990)

C Loscalzo, 'Ephesians 4:1-16,' *Rev. Expo.* 85 (1988): pp 687-91

P T O'Brien, *The Letter to the Ephesians*, The Pillar New Testament Commentary (Grand Rapids, MI: Eerdmans, 1999)

J C O'Neill, '"The Work of the Ministry" in Ephesians 4:12 and the New Testament,' *Expo. Times* 112 (2001), pp 336-40

J Piper, *Brothers, We Are Not Professionals: A Plea to Pastors for Radical Ministry*, 2nd ed. (Nashville: Broadman & Holman, 2013)

D W B Robinson, 'Ministry/service in the Bible: Human and Divine, Secular and Sacred,' pp 51-64 in *Forward in Faith? Proceedings of the 1996 Conference of the Association for the Apostolic Ministry (Australia)* (Enmore: Aquila Books (Australia), 1998)

———, 'Who Were "the Saints"?,' *Reform. Theol. Rev.* 22, no. 2 (1963), pp 45-53

E Schweizer, *Church Order in the New Testament*, Studies in Biblical theology 32 (London: SCM, 1971)

M Silva, *Biblical Words and Their Meaning: An Introduction to Lexical Semantics*, revised and expanded ed. (Grand Rapids: Zondervan, 1994)

C S Smith, 'Unchanged "Teaching": The Meaning of *Didaskō* in 1 Timothy 2:12,' *Women, Sermons and the Bible: Essays Interacting with John Dickson's Hearing Her Voice*, edited by Peter G Bolt and Tony Payne, Kindle (Matthias Media, 2014)

F Thielman, *Ephesians*, Baker Exegetical Commentary on the New Testament (Grand Rapids: Baker, 2010)

L J Windsor, *Paul and the Vocation of Israel: How Paul's Jewish Identity Informs His Apostolic Ministry, with Special Reference to Romans*, BZNW 205 (Berlin: De Gruyter, 2014)

2. The Sufficient Word – *Mark D Thompson*

Twenty years ago this year, the American preacher and pastor, John MacArthur Jr, wrote '*Sola Scriptura* simply means that all truth necessary for our salvation and spiritual life is taught either explicitly or implicitly in Scripture'.[1] In putting it this way, he was remarkably close to the concerns of 39 Articles, which emphasise both the authority and the sufficiency of Holy Scripture. Not that the Articles were unconcerned with the origin or the truthfulness or the clarity of Scripture, which they affirm in other ways (and these certainly are addressed in the Homily entitled 'A Fruitful Exhortation to the Reading and Knowledge of Holy Scripture'); but the Articles are primarily concerned with the supreme authority and the sufficiency of the Old and New Testaments. 'Holy Scripture containeth all things necessary to salvation: so that whatsoever is not read therein, nor may be proved thereby, is not to be required of any man, that it should be believed as an article of the Faith, or be thought requisite or necessary to salvation'.[2]

The sufficiency of Scripture is, then, a key Protestant conviction. It is not everything that is to be said about *sola scriptura,* and to this extent at least MacArthur's definition is inadequate. *Sola scriptura* also speaks about Scripture as the final authority which stands alone above all other authorities. But the sufficiency of Scripture is a very important part of the confession of *sola scriptura.* All the more so when we consider the context in which the confession was made. The Roman Church of the sixteenth century emphasised the importance of the church's voice as an interpreter of Scripture and a supplement to Scripture. The Scriptures were not in themselves sufficient to establish doctrine, or direct piety, or settle disputes, or provide access to the saving grace of Christ. Without the church the Scripture remained a dark and obscure word. But God has given us the church to enable us to use Scripture rightly and access all its benefits. And through the church we receive grace: 'outside the church there is no salvation' (*extra ecclesiam nulla salus*). Against that background it is not hard to see why Cranmer and the convocation of Canterbury drafted Article VI the way they did.

---

1 J MacArthur Jr, 'The Sufficiency of the Written Word', in *Sola Scriptura: The Protestant Position on the Bible* (Morgan, PA: Soli Deo Gloria, 1995), p 165.

2 Article VI.

But what did they really mean? It is all too easy for *sola scriptura* to morph into what has been variously labelled *solo scriptura* or *nuda scriptura*.[3] Forgetting that the Reformers wrote with copious reference to the church fathers, the creeds of the ancient church, and even some of the medieval writers, it is sometimes suggested that we need no theologians other than the Bible writers, no knowledge other than that contained in Scripture, in order to live fruitfully and faithfully in the last days. Often appeal is made to William Chillingworth (1602–1644) in this connection. In his book *The Religion of Protestants a Safe Way to Salvation* (1637), he wrote, 'The Bible, I say, the Bible only, is the Religion of Protestants'.[4] It is always possible to caricature someone by just quoting a single line out of context. And the context of Chillingworth's comment is important. He was entering into a debate between Christopher Potter, the Protestant Provost of The Queen's College Oxford, and a Jesuit apologist named Edward Knott. Perhaps if we look a little more extensively at what Chillingworth actually said in context we might not be so quick to write him off as an extremist:

> Know then Sir, that when I say the Religion of Protestants is in prudence to be preferr'd before yours; as on the one side, I do not understand by your Religion the Doctrin of *Bellarmin,* or *Baronins,* or any other private man among you, nor the Doctrin of the *Sorbon,* or of the *Jesuits,* or of the *Dominicans,* or of any other particular company among you, but that wherein you all agree, or profess to agree, *the Doctrin of the Council of Trent;* so accordingly on the other side, by the *Religion of Protestants,* I do not understand the Doctrin of *Luther,* or *Calvin,* or *Melancthon,* nor the confession of *Augusta,* or *Geneva,* nor the Catechism of *Heidelberg,* nor the Articles of the Church of *England,* No nor the *Harmony* of Protestant Confessions; but that wherein they all agree, and which they all subscribe with a greater Harmony, as a perfect rule of their faith and actions, that is, the BIBLE. The BIBLE, I say, the BIBLE only, is the Religion of Protestants! Whatsoever else they believe besides it, and the plain, irrefragable, indubitable consequences of it, well may they hold it as a matter of Opinion; but as a matter of Faith and Religion, neither can they with coherence to their own grounds believe it themselves,

---

3 For the first, see Kevin Vanhoozer's soon to be published lectures on *Mere Protestantism*; for the second, Tony Lane's article on *sola scriptura* in *A Pathway into the Holy Scripture*, ed. P E Satterthwaite & D F Wright (Grand Rapids: Eerdmans, 1994), p 327.

4 W Chillingworth, *The Works of William Chillingworth Containing his book The Religion of Protestants a Safe Way to Salvation*, (London: Motte, 1719), p 271.

> nor require the belief of it of others, without most high and most schismatical presumption.[5]

Just a few lines later he gives his more measured conclusion.

> 'I am full assured that God does not, and therefore that man ought not to, require any more of any man than this, to believe the Scripture to be God's word, and to endeavour to find the true sense of it, and to live according to it.'[6]

Not even Chillingworth, in the end, was a consistent exponent of *solo scriptura* or *nuda scriptura*. He worked and wrote within the fellowship of the saints, read and cited those who had wrestled with Scripture before him, but all the while maintaining that they had no claim on his conscience in the way that Scripture did. He knew the Bible didn't say everything about everything; but it said what mattered and it stood alone in a position to establish doctrine, or direct piety or settle disputes, or provide access to the saving grace of Christ. And he clearly believed that the Bible directed you to faith in Christ, and not faith in the Bible itself, as the means of salvation.

All of this is not surprising of course. Luther and Calvin, both stalwarts of *sola scriptura*, regularly cited other authorities, though none of them were final; and neither of them restricted themselves to only the words on the scriptural page. Luther's famous stand at Worms is a case in point: 'Unless I am convinced by the testimony of the Holy Scriptures or by evident reason' – by which he meant legitimate argument from Scripture; but he did not stop there – 'I consider myself convicted by the testimony of Holy Scripture, which is my basis; my conscience is captive to the Word of God'.[7] Luther recognised and used other authorities and made what he considered were justifiable inferences from explicit words of Scripture, but his conscience was captive to the Word of God – and there is no doubt that at this point, as elsewhere, the Word of God was for Luther, Holy Scripture.

---

5 Chilllingworth, *Works*, p 271.

6 Chillingworth, *Works*, p 272.

7 M Luther, 'The Account and Actions of Doctor Martin Luther the Augustinian at the Diet of Worms (1521)', in *Luther's Works* (54 vols; St Louis/Minneapolis: Concordia/Fortress, 1955–86), 32:112.

2.1. *What do we mean by 'sufficient'?*

So what do we really mean by the *sufficiency* of Scripture? I well remember one of my lecturers at Moore College in the 1980s, probably one you'd never expect, explaining in a lecture on ministry that 'we want you to develop the habit, and conscientiously to be committed to, bringing the teaching of the Bible to bear in every pastoral situation ... Whenever we gather, we open God's word, confident that God addresses us in whatever situation we might find ourselves.' So whether in a church building on Sunday, in a living room during the week, at a bedside, at a graveside, at a church business meeting, wherever, Christian ministry is a ministry of prayer and the word. But how far does that extend? What do we really mean by the sufficiency of the written word of God?

It might seem transparently obvious, but 'sufficient' is an incomplete predicate. To say something is 'sufficient' is to beg the question 'sufficient for what?' And what is the basis of this claim of sufficiency anyhow? In the remainder of this chapter I want to look briefly at just what we mean by sufficiency and our grounds for making such a claim and then to look at two test cases: our ministry of preaching and teaching the word and the practice of pastoral counselling.

It has most likely already occurred to you that for the claim of Scripture's sufficiency to have any coherence, it must itself arise from the teaching of Scripture itself. And without a doubt your mind will have travelled to the classic text in the New Testament which is the reference point for all theological discussions of Scripture's sufficiency or perfection, as some call it: 2 Timothy 3:14-17.

> But as for you, continue in what you have learned and have firmly believed, knowing from whom you learned it and how from childhood you have been acquainted with the sacred writings, which are able to make you wise for salvation through faith in Christ Jesus. All Scripture is breathed out by God and profitable for teaching, for reproof, for correction and for training in righteousness, that the man of God may be competent, equipped for every good work.

Straightaway it is possible to identify the kind of sufficiency Paul had in mind in these verses. First, the Scriptures are able to make you 'wise for salvation through faith in Christ Jesus'. This is where you find what you need to know about the salvation God offers to you in Christ. This is where you are introduced to the true Christ who gives real salvation and through his Spirit engenders faith. Here is the proper anchor for faith, 'faith in Christ Jesus'.

Secondly, through the means of teaching, reproof, correction and training in righteousness, the Christian leader is equipped for every good work. The same Scriptures which introduce us to Christ and the salvation that can be had in him, prepare his people to live as his people in the world. A critical word is the word ἄρτιος, translated 'competent' in the *ESV*. Marshall notes how the word means 'complete, capable, proficient'.[8] Louw and Nida speak of being 'qualified', something like 'having all that is necessary to meet whatever demands are put upon him'.[9] This sense is strengthened by the participle ἐξηρτισμένος, which the *ESV* translates simply as 'equipped'. It is a word used elsewhere of the 'completion' of Paul's stay in the city of Tyre on the way to Jerusalem (Acts 21:5). The sense is clearly very close to what we mean by sufficiency: all that is needed to be 'put into full working order',[10] is provided by the Scriptures. What the Christian leader needs in order to be able to 'do those good works which God prepared beforehand, that we should walk in them' (Ephesians 2:10) is given in the God-breathed Scriptures.

One of the most extensive meditations on these verses, and their import, is found in the treatment of Scripture's 'perfection' by the Genevan theologian François Turretin (1623–1687). Turretin's way of doing theology, his question and answer technique with all its resonances of Aquinas, is not in vogue today. His approach is light years away from the 'I' theology of Stanley Hauerwas,[11] or the erudite, if sometimes a little abstract, discourse of John Webster.[12] Most of us would find him far less engaging than the creative and sometimes playful explorations of Kevin Vanhoozer.[13] But there is gold in them there hills! And as he meditates on what it means, and what it does not mean, to say that Scripture is perfect – in the sense of complete or sufficient – he has some worthwhile things to say.

---

8 I H Marshall & P H Towner, *The Pastoral Epistles* (ICC; Edinburgh: T. & T. Clark, 1999), p 796.

9 J P Louw & E A Nida, *Greek-English Lexicon of the New Testament based on Semantic Domains* (Broadway, NY: UBS, 1988), p 679.

10 Marshall & Towner, *Pastoral Epistles*, p 796.

11 S Hauerwas, *The Work of Theology* (Grand Rapids: Eerdmans, 2015), pp 19-27.

12 J Webster, 'Theological Theology', *Confessing God: Essays in Christian Dogmatics II* (London: T. & T. Clark, 2005), pp 11-31.

13 K J Vanhoozer, *Biblical Authority after Babel: Retrieving the Solas in the Spirit of Mere Protestant Christianity* (Grand Rapids: Eerdmans, 2016 [October] – forthcoming).

In seeking to be precise in what he is talking about, Turretin insists:

> the question is not whether the scriptures contain all those things which were said or done by Christ and the saints or have any connection whatever to do with religion ... the question relates only to things necessary to salvation – whether they belong to faith or to practice; whether all these things are so contained in the Scriptures that they can be a total and adequate rule of faith and practice ...[14]

There are strict limits to our claim that Scripture is sufficient: what is necessary for salvation in both faith and practice – how we are saved and how we are to live as those who are saved. Turretin will acknowledge there are things that are not explicit in Scripture but which by legitimate inference can be said to be taught by Scripture. The full-orbed doctrine of the Trinity is one of those: three equal and eternal 'persons' without ever being three gods or merely three faces of the one God. This confession is latent in Scripture. It is not explicit, at least not explicit in that kind of detail. However, the doctrine of the Trinity is a fair and legitimate inference from the way Scripture speaks of the Father and the Son and the Holy Spirit. It is not something we *add to* Scripture.

Turretin will also acknowledge that traditions of various kinds are helpful but tradition does not determine matters of doctrine or morals. There are various authorities in the various areas of life. Their voices are not silenced by the Scriptures necessarily, but they are certainly relativised. There are various traditions and frameworks of thinking. These are real and bring real benefit. But in the area of doctrine and morals all other traditions and ways of thinking and behaving are brought under the scrutiny, evaluation and authority of the Scriptures.

Here, then, is Turretin's conclusion:

> The question then amounts to this – whether the Scripture perfectly contains all things (not absolutely), but necessary to salvation; not expressly and in so many words, but equivalently and by legitimate inference, as to leave no place for any unwritten word containing doctrinal or moral traditions.[15]

Then, turning to 2 Timothy 3:15-16 Turretin identifies at least three latent arguments for the perfection of Scripture in this passage.

First, the Holy Scriptures 'are able to make us wise unto salvation'

---

[14] F Turretin, *Institutes of Elenctic Theology*, trans. G M Giger; ed. J T Dennison; (Phillipsburg: P& R, 1992 [1679]), p 135.

[15] Turretin, *Institutes*, p 136.

> (2 Timothy 3:15). For what do we desire more than to be made partakers of salvation? Second, it is useful for all theoretical and practical purposes, for teaching the faith and forming the manners. Third, it can make the man or minister of God perfect in every good work, and what is sufficient for the shepherd must also be so for the sheep.[16]

Turretin's is a bold and somewhat lengthy statement of the perfection or sufficiency of Scripture, but in answering this question he spends an entire paragraph (para. XX[7]) citing the opinions of the church fathers on this matter – Tertullian, Jerome, Augustine, Basil and Irenaeus. This is not inconsistency, precisely because of the way Turretin has limited the notion of sufficiency in the first place. Scripture determines what we believe and how we are to live as Christ's saved people; and this has always been the testimony of Christians. That testimony is itself a confirmation, not supplanting the teaching of Scripture but confirming it.

There is one other thing worth noticing in Turretin before we leave him behind. As he heads down the home stretch in his description of Scripture's perfection, he writes,

> The perfection of Scripture asserted by us does not exclude either the ecclesiastical ministry (established by God for the setting forth and application of the word) or the internal power of the Holy Spirit necessary for conversion. It only excludes the necessity of another rule for external direction added to the Scriptures to make them perfect. A rule is not therefore imperfect because it requires the hand of the architect for its application.[17]

Not me alone with the Bible, deciding for myself what it means and how it applies, but me standing within the God-given gift of the Christian fellowship, and endowed by the Spirit by which God has brought me to new life, finding that this word does indeed prepare me to be Christ's man or woman in the world for whom Christ died.

Just a generation later, as it all began to go pear-shaped in the Genevan Academy, one of Turretin's orthodox successors, Benedict Pictet (1655–1724), gave a very similar account of the sufficiency of Scripture, but provided some additional clarification:

---

16 Turretin, *Institutes*, p 136.

17 Turretin, *Institutes*, p 141.

1. There are some things necessary to salvation which are naturally known to all, as the existence of God, the immortality of the soul, &c. it is not necessary that these truths should be professed taught in the scriptures. They must be taken for granted, and not proved ...
2. All things necessary to salvation are not taught in scripture in express words, nor was it needful; but some are expressly laid down, others are deduced by fair and legitimate inferences.
3. This perfection also is confined to those things which are necessary to salvation, for it was not God's design in giving us the scriptures, to make us philosophers, or mathematicians, or physcians, &c.
4. Traditions may be of some use, both for the illustration of scriptural passages, and for the defence of the truth, provided they be subjected to the authority of scripture and be reckoned amongst things merely human.[18]

The point is that even in the heyday of *sola scriptura*, and even amongst those who sought to defend with the utmost clarity and passion the sufficiency of Scripture on the basis of 2 Timothy 3 at the very least, this incomplete predication has been filled out with qualifications in both directions. In one direction, the Scriptures do not tell us everything about everything. They are not in any absolute sense the sole repository of truth. It is possible to push the confession of the sufficiency of Scripture too far. And repeatedly the way of avoiding this trap has been to insist Scripture is entirely sufficient 'in all things necessary for salvation'. It will address other issues, and when it does so it is certainly authoritative, for example Christian marriage and how we ought to treat one another in the Christian congregation. But other knowledge will have a role here that it does not have on the issue of how I am saved and how I live as a saved person. John's Gospel provides an interesting test case. John himself declares that he has written what he has written 'so that you may believe that Jesus is the Christ, the Son of God, and that by believing you may have life in his name' (John 20:31). John's Gospel touches on a lot of other things and has authoritative things to say about those things, but the purpose for which it was written and for which it is entirely sufficient is to provide the ground for belief.

---

18 B Pictet, *Christian Theology*, trans. F Reyroux; (Weston Green: Seeley and Sons, 1833 [1696]), pp 43, 44, 46.

In the other direction, it is just as possible to be satisfied with a watered down account of the sufficiency of Scripture which pays little attention to the distinctive character of the Scriptures as the God-breathed word. There is a qualitative difference between the Bible and all other theological writing. Augustine recognized that long ago when, in his tract on Baptism he acknowledged the inerrancy of Scripture and its distinction from 'all later letters of bishops'.[19] Scripture is not only the touchstone against which all other doctrinal and moral writing is to be tested, it alone binds the Christian's conscience – to return to Luther again.

Contemporary evangelical Christianity appears to be challenged in these two diametrically opposed directions. On one hand, there is a troubling repudiation of systematic theology and the need of anything other than the Bible and my own exegetical skills to live the Christian life and conduct Christian ministry in today's world. This is, in some measure, a reaction to the way theological systems can ride roughshod over the Bible and we can become partisans of a particular theological position rather than subjecting all theological traditions to the scrutiny of Scripture itself. In response it is worth remembering that Scripture alone is indeed the final authority but that does not mean there are no other authorities. At the time of the Reformation, the people who rejected everything and wanted to start again, just them with the Bible, were the Anabaptist radicals who created havoc in Europe. Without the discipline of the communion of saints, stretching back through time as well as across space, without recognising we are not the first to read Scripture and seek to live in the light of its teaching, we can simply repeat the mistakes of the past, or worse still simply indulge our own idiosyncratic readings of Scripture without realising how much we are influenced by our own time, our own culture, our own predispositions. The same Spirit who moved the prophets and apostles to write gathers us into the fellowship of Christ's people, gifts some to teach (by speaking and by writing), and has ensured we have the entire canon and not just part of it.

On the other hand, there is an equally troubling exaltation of the theological tradition and a naivety in the face of the world's claims to truth. A renewed focus on the claims of the world and contemporary culture is sometimes justified with a rather Kuyperian view of common grace. The biblical teaching that God 'makes his sun rise on the evil and

---

19 Augustine, *On Baptism*, in P Schaff (ed.) *The Nicene and Post-Nicene Fathers* (Grand Rapids: Eerdmans, 1979, IV), II.3.

on the good, and sends rain on the just and on the unjust' (Matthew 5:45) underwent considerable hypotrophy in the thought of the Dutch theologian and politician Abraham Kuyper (1837–1920) in the late nineteenth and early twentieth century in part to justify a more positive engagement with human culture. While Kuyper and his fellow countryman Herman Bavinck (1854–1921) preserved a distinction between common grace and saving grace, in later generations that is not always so clear. The world can speak the truth of God; the world can even exercise a spiritual ministry to us because of God's common grace.

The new prominence being given to tradition by some evangelicals is in part a response to the hubristic dismissal of centuries of exegetical and theological endeavour in the name of *sola scriptura*. Isn't there much to learn from those who have wrestled with these questions before us? Yet this renewed interest in 'the theological tradition' (which operates as an umbrella term covering a number of theological traditions) runs the risk of diverting attention from the subject of the conversation to the conversation itself. I'm reminded of Karl Barth's comment that the angels laugh at 'the men who write so much about Karl Barth instead of writing about the things he is trying to write about'.[20] Such a shift of focus is disturbing since the more attention given to tradition alongside Scripture, the greater the danger that tradition will be allowed to speak instead of Scripture. To use Heiko Oberman's categories, Tradition I, tradition as simply reiterating the teaching of Scripture, can so easily slip into becoming Tradition II, tradition as supplementing and even subverting the teaching of Scripture.[21]

So what has all this to do with pastoral ministry? Let me turn then to the practice of preaching as a first test case.

2.2. *The sufficient word and preaching*

How might the sufficiency of the word shape and express itself in the preaching ministry exercised within the churches? In most evangelical churches there is a formal commitment to biblical preaching, built upon a conviction that God addresses his people as his word is expounded. However, there is an even more profound connection between

---

20 Quoted by Johannes A Lombard in G Casalis, *Portrait of Karl Barth*, trans. R McAfee Brown; (Garden City, NY: Anchor, 1964), p 3.

21 H A Oberman, *Forerunners of the Reformation: The Shape of Late Medieval thought* (London: Lutterworth, 1967), p 58.

preaching and the Scripture both as forms of the word of God. Luther's threefold form of the word of God, and Karl Barth's twentieth century modification of this idea as a reflection of God's triune nature, come to mind. Both provide a rationale for referring to preaching as well as to Scripture as 'the word of God'. The apostle Paul could give thanks that the Thessalonians received the word of God which they had heard from him and his friends, accepting it not as the word of men but 'as what it really is, the word of God, which is at work in you believers' (1 Thessalonians 2:13).

Preaching, as Paul understood it, is considerably more than simply reading Scripture out loud. Paul insisted that Timothy devote himself not only to the public reading (τῇ ἀναγνώσει) of Scripture but also to exhortation (τῇ παρακλήσει) and to teaching (τῇ διδασκαλίᾳ). There is a difference between a literary analysis of a biblical text and a Christian sermon. Of course there are various types of preaching: expository preaching, textual preaching, doctrinal preaching, topical preaching and the rest. Each represents a different way of dealing with the biblical text and dealing with those being addressed by that text today. Yet each involves not only description but exhortation, each draws explicit connection between the teaching of Scripture and the circumstances of the hearers, what we might call application. Preaching at its best exposes both the heart of the text and the text of our hearts.

The underlying assumption is that what we need to hear is not human speculations about God but God's revealed plan and will for us. We need to see God's Christ for who he is and from that great vantage point re-evaluate everything else. It is in Scripture that we hear what God has done, the proper ground of faith. It is in Scripture that we hear how we should respond to such grace, mercy and love, in repentance and faith. God is sovereign over the reception of Scripture just as he was sovereign over the origin of Scripture. As Jesus explained to his disciples in the wake of his teaching about parables: 'to you has been *given* the secret of the kingdom of God, but for those outside everything is in parables, so that they may indeed see but not perceive, and may indeed hear but not understand, lest they should turn and be forgiven' (Mark 4:11-12). God will accomplish with his word what he set out to do with it (Isaiah 55:10-11). In some cases it will be salvation; in others it will be judgment.

Evangelicals, especially under the influence of people like John Stott and Dick Lucas in the UK, and John Chapman and Dudley Foord in Australia, have long regarded the systematic exposition of passages of

Scripture as the appropriate core diet of a Christian congregation. It allows God to set the agenda. Not that other kinds of preaching are necessarily illegitimate. But expository preaching prevents us from just preaching the parts we like and avoiding those which are less palatable or less likely to gain us praise. It teaches people how to read the Bible for themselves. A former archbishop of Sydney once said, quite some time ago, 'Whenever you teach the Bible you are really doing two things. You are teaching what this passage is saying – or you should be – and you are teaching how to read the Bible. And over time your people will read the Bible the way their pastor preaches the Bible.' It is undoubtedly true. So, what are you teaching your church or Bible Study group or whatever about how to read the Bible?

The doctrine of the sufficiency of Scripture functions to strengthen the Bible teacher's confidence that God is at work and will do his work among his people. The Bible does not need to be supplemented. It doesn't need to be *made* relevant. It already is. But it is also my job as a teacher or preacher to help clear away the roadblocks which keep members of the congregation from recognising and responding to the prior and continuing relevance of God's word. Through this word God is still drawing men and women to himself. Through this word he is still building men and women into the likeness of Christ.

How might our preaching compromise this principle of the sufficiency of Scripture? How might our preaching betray our own lack of confidence that Scripture is sufficient – because if we are not convinced it is sufficient, then those we preach to surely will not be.

I could certainly be wrong, but I think I discern a number of changes to preaching in at least some of our churches over the last ten years, each of which have the potential to do just this. A friend of mine who attends an Anglican church in our diocese commented to me not that long ago that she did not take her Bible to church any more because she did not need it. Whereas when she first went to this church people were encouraged to open their Bibles and a particular passage would be explained and applied, in more recent years the Bible passage was merely a launching pad as the preacher identified an idea and then preached the rest of the sermon on the idea, not on the passage.

If this change really is widespread, then I suspect it is due, at least in part, to the influence of some popular American preachers, whose use of the biblical text is not unlike the springboard approach: start with a biblical text but leave the text behind as you spend most of the time thinking and talking about how the central idea is reflected in, or challenges, thought and behaviour in our world. Perhaps it is also borne out of a certain boredom with the traditional diet of expounding one passage after another – particularly if we are predictable and heavy handed in our application of biblical theology. I remember an English friend of mine complaining about how many of the sermons he hears all sound the same – moving from this particular passage to Jesus in the same way all the time, with the same general and rather banal applications to the lives of those who are listening. 'Ten thousand, thousand are their texts, but all their sermons one.'[22]

The second change I see is the rise and dominance of apologetic preaching. The questions of the world are setting the agenda for the preaching rather than a systematic engagement with the unfolding story of the Bible. I'm not talking about the occasional sermon or sermon series that addresses a pressing issue of the moment, giving people the biblical resources to assess what is happening around them and to speak into their world when the opportunity arises. That is a good and important garnish to the main meal. Rather, I'm talking about when the sermons are consistently dominated by our social analysis or by the questions of those outside the household of faith.

I think it is worth asking ourselves just what it is that we expect will be the real power for lasting change in our hearers. Is our confidence really that the word of God is powerful to transform lives? Or is our confidence more obviously in our own astute social commentary, as we insightfully analyse the movements of the moment? Or do we think that the real change will be effected by, or as a result of, the emotional or spiritual moment you are striving to create by your use of language, stories and the like?

Of course, serious reflection upon the world into which we are preaching, illuminating illustration, and engaging, carefully crafted language all have an important role in preaching and teaching. Application is essential – though it doesn't always have to be something *I do*. But if we believe in the sufficient word, if we believe that it is the word of God that brings real life-long change in his people, we will recognise that these are aids and confirmations and supports, not the driving force of the sermon.

---

[22] G Goldsworthy, *Preaching the Whole Bible as Christian Scripture: The Application of Biblical Theology to Expository Preaching* (Grand Rapids: Eerdmans, 2000), p 126.

2.3. *The sufficient word and pastoral counselling*

The second test case is the biblical counselling movement. There is, you might be aware, a vast literature on this. How do we approach the task of assisting people to think through the circumstances of their lives, and particularly the struggles they are facing, in a Christian way? Is the Bible really sufficient for this purpose? Should we, and if we should, how should we, integrate the insights of modern psychology? Are these the equivalent of 'the other secondary authorities' which serve in theology but always under the scrutiny and authority of Scripture? Is the care of Christian people the sole province of the pastor or should we involve the particular skills and knowledge of trained clinical psychologists? And if we were to do that, would we be jeopardising our conviction that Scripture is sufficient for life as God's person in God's world?

One of the most influential writers in the biblical counselling movement has been Jay E Adams, who is still alive at the ripe old age of 86. Another writer in the area of ministry and pastoral care, Derek Tidball, who as a matter of fact strongly disagrees with Adams at points, concedes that 'Jay Adams has, without doubt, made an enormous contribution to the revival of a biblical pastoral theology'.[23] Adams really came to notice through his book *Competent to Counsel,* which was published in 1970.[24] In it he introduced the notion of 'nouthetic counselling', an approach dominated by three ideas: confrontation, concern and change. In Adam's own words, 'nouthetic counselling consists of lovingly confronting people out of deep concern in order to help them make those changes that God requires'.[25] He continues, 'The nouthetic counsellor believes that all that is needed to help another person love God and his neighbour as he should, as the verse above indicates [he has just quoted 2 Timothy 3:16-17], may be found in the Bible ... Biblical counselling is done by Christians who are convinced that God is able to make the changes that are necessary as His Word is ministered in the power of the Spirit'.[26]

Adams is certainly a person committed to the sufficiency of Scripture but in a way, I suggest, that goes beyond the way this doctrine

---

[23] D Tidball, *Skilful Shepherds: Explorations in Pastoral Theology* (Leicester: IVP, 1986), p 238.

[24] J E Adams, *Competent to Counsel* (Grand Rapids: Zondervan, 1970).

[25] J E Adams, 'What is "Nouthetic" Counseling?' online at Institute for Nouthetic Studies http://www.nouthetic.org/about-ins/what-is-nouthetic-counseling (accessed 9 September 2015).

[26] Adams, 'What is "Nouthetic" Counseling?'

has normally been understood. Does the sufficiency of Scripture extend to every issue we face? Is the Bible a manual for every aspect of life covering every circumstance? Is all psychology really from the devil, as some of Adams' followers seem to imply? Jay Adams is undoubtedly right to raise questions about the presuppositions and the methods of Sigmund Freud, Carl Jung and Carl Rogers. There is a fundamental difference between a humanist worldview and the worldview of those who know themselves to be redeemed and deeply loved creatures of a personal Creator. But are there no insights at all to gain about the way we function in the world, marred and broken as we all are, from the discipline of psychology? Does that really fit with the way God has made the world with its own real but contingent intelligibility, where you can make sense of the world on its own terms even if this is not the whole story? If the sufficiency of Scripture relates specifically to 'all things necessary for salvation', might there not be other things, that are not strictly speaking 'necessary for salvation' where Scripture is not sufficient, even in human life and relationships? Might there not be other claims to wisdom which should not be dismissed outright but be tested for their compatibility with Scripture?

Adams has important things to say and important correctives to make to a culture besotted with 'therapy'. But his approach is not the only one in this area and not the only one claiming to uphold the sufficiency of Scripture. One important review of the Biblical counselling movement 'after Adams' insists 'though some believe that there has been disagreement among counsellors concerning Scripture's sufficiency, in truth this is one of the main areas in which there has been no change in the last twenty years'.[27] Larry Crabb, for instance, takes a different approach to that of Adams but still insists on the sufficiency of Scripture. His way of putting this is:

> Yes, the Bible is sufficient, because it provides either direct information or authoritative categories for answering all questions about how life should be lived on this earth and about how it can be lived according to an effective pattern. Whenever the Bible is not explicit about a given concern, biblical categories provide a framework for thinking through an adequate response to that concern.[28]

---

[27] H Lambert, *The Biblical Counselling Movement After Adams* (Wheaton: Crossway, 2012), p 137.

[28] L J Crabb, *Understanding People: Deep Longings for Relationship* (Melbourne: Bacon, 1987), p 47.

Crabb's difficulty with Adams' nouthetic approach is that it doesn't go deep enough. He outlines two specific reservations:

1. It is possible to give the literal meaning of the text a comprehensive relevance that it simply does not have.
2. When the range of permissible questions is narrowed [to those the Bible specifically answers] our understanding of complicated problems tends to become simplistic.[29]

And it should be said that Crabb does this after distinguishing two categories of problems: those resulting from physical/natural causes and those resulting from fundamentally moral causes.[30] This is a very helpful distinction which merits serious attention.

Scripture is able to make us wise to salvation through faith in Christ Jesus. It is able to equip us for life and ministry in the world God has made but where life at every level is under strain because of human sin. We must certainly say that the deepest cause of our disorder, whatever form that disorder might take, is our complicity in the human rebellion against the rule and love of the one who made us. The impact of the Fall, and our orientation to the autonomy and independence offered by the fruit in the Garden, goes very deep. And we must bring the teaching of Scripture to bear on this situation. Adams and Crabb agree on this point. But the problems this situation creates exist on many levels and some are not directly addressed by the Scriptures. Clinical depression, with deeply ingrained patterns of thinking and/or chemical imbalance in the brain, sometimes itself one of the scars of trauma or abuse, is a case in point. The Bible has a lot to say about how we ought to think about ourselves and God and the world around us. It challenges self-loathing just as it challenges self-exaltation. But it says little about how to help a person caught in that spiral by the other factors I have mentioned. So with a careful eye on what Scripture does actually say, and the categories it provides for making sense of life in the world before God, we might gladly embrace the knowledge of human psychology God has graciously granted to others.

I am quite aware I have only just scratched the surface on this topic, and I do so as someone who has not made biblical counselling a research specialty. There is undoubtedly more to say. But I would suggest that *both* neglecting the Scripture's diagnosis of our most fundamental problem *and* refusing to access the expertise of those with

---

29 Crabb, *Understanding People*, pp 55, 57.

30 Crabb, *Understanding People*, p 46.

professional training in this area where necessary can cause incalculable damage.

2.4. *Conclusion*

The Protestant conviction that the Bible is sufficient 'in all things necessary for salvation' and that it is 'able to make you wise for salvation through faith in Christ Jesus' is something that needs to be taken with renewed seriousness in our current climate. I am glad to have developed that conscience my old lecturer was hoping for, trusting that what people need to hear most of all is the word of God and so turning to it in large groups and small one-to-one meetings and in a whole host of circumstances. But it is possible to abuse the Bible in more than one way, and one we must be wary of in this connection is pressing the Scriptures into service in areas where they were not intended to serve.

So the question to ask whatever aspect of pastoral ministry I am engaged in is this: is my practice demonstrating confidence in God's provision for his people in his written word? Am I encouraging my colleagues and friends and those I serve to take seriously the sufficiency of Scripture? Am I encouraging the testing of all things against this unwavering standard, recognising what God has given in a myriad of other ways but determined in my commitment that it is only here, in these words, that I hear God's authoritative explanation of himself, his purposes and his perspective on my life and my future?

2.5. *Bibliography*

J E Adams, *Competent to Counsel* (Grand Rapids: Zondervan, 1970)

———, 'What is "Nouthetic" Counseling?', online at *Institute for Nouthetic Studies* http://www.nouthetic.org/about-ins/what-is-nouthetic-counseling (accessed 9 September 2015)

Augustine, *On Baptism*, in P. Schaff (ed), *The Nicene and Post-Nicene Fathers* IV (Grand Rapids: Eerdmans, 1979)

G Casalis, *Portrait of Karl Barth*, R. McAfee Brown (trans.); (Garden City, NY: Anchor, 1964)

W Chillingworth, *The Works of William Chillingworth Containing his book entitled The Religion of Protestants a Safe Way to Salvation.* (Repr. London: Motte, 1719 [1637])

L Crabb, *Understanding People: Deep Longings for Relationship* (Grand Rapids: Zondervan, 1987)

G L Goldsworthy, *Preaching the whole Bible as Christian Scripture: The Application of Biblical Theology to Expository Preaching* (Grand Rapids: Eerdmans, 2000)

S Hauerwas, *The Work of Theology* (Grand Rapids: Eerdmans, 2015)

H Lambert, *The Biblical Counselling Movement after Adams* (Wheaton: Crossway, 2012)

A N S Lane, '*Sola Scriptura?* Making Sense of a Post-Reformation Slogan', in P E Satterthwaite & D F Wright (eds), *A Pathway into the Holy Scripture* (Grand Rapids: Eerdmans, 1994)

J P Louw, & E A Nida, *Greek-English Lexicon of the New Testament based on Semantic Domains* (Broadway, NY: United Bible Societies, 1988)

M Luther, 'The Account and Actions of Doctor Martin Luther the Augustinian at the Diet of Worms', in *Luther's Works*; 54 vols; (St Louis/Minneapolis: Concordia/Fortress, 1955–86 [1521]), 32:105-131.

J F MacArthur, 'The Sufficiency of the Written Word: Answering the Roman Catholic Apologists', in D Kistler (ed.), *Sola Scriptura: The Protestant Position on the Bible* (Morgan, PA: Soli Deo Gloria, 1995)

I H Marshall & P H Towner, *The Pastoral* Epistles; ICC; (Edinburgh: T. & T. Clark, 1999)

H A Oberman, *Forerunners of the Reformation: The Shape of Late Medieval Thought* (London: Lutterworth, 1967)

B Pictet, *Christian Theology*; F Revroux (trans.); (Weston Green, Seeley and Sons, 1833 [1696])

D Tidball, *Skilful Shepherds: Explorations in Pastoral Theology* (Leicester: IVP, 1986)

F Turretin, *Institutes of Elenctic Theology: Volume 1 First through Tenth Topics*; G M Giger (trans.); J T Dennison (ed.); 3 vols; (Phillipsburg: P & R, 1992 [1679])

K J Vanhoozer, *Biblical Authority after Babel: Retrieving the Solas in the Spirit of Mere Protestant Christianity* (Grand Rapids: Eerdmans, 2016 [October])

J Webster, 'Theological Theology', *Confessing God* (London: T. & T. Clark, 2005)

3. Pastoral Preaching – *David Peterson*

The sermon was based on a passage in Deuteronomy. The preacher spent a long time describing the context of the passage in the Pentateuch, but little time explaining the text itself. The outline revealed that it was effectively a topical sermon, with illustrations that did not really touch on the profound theological meaning of the passage. Was it a good example of pastoral preaching? Not if it purported to use the Bible to address a pastoral issue in the congregation. Moreover, the pastoral issue was really swamped by too much attention to unnecessary background information.

Getting the right balance between context, exegesis, theological analysis, and pastoral application is difficult. But it is a blend we need to keep trying to achieve, if we wish to use the Bible appropriately, and to minister to the real needs of people in our care.

3.1. *Ephesian models*

3.1.1. *Addressing the elders*

We don't really have any sermons directed to Christian congregations in the New Testament. However, Paul's address to the Ephesian elders in Acts 20:17-35 opens an important window for us. The apostle charged these leaders to shepherd the church of God with faithful teaching. In so doing, he used a number of key terms to describe his own ministry among them.

These terms describe his evangelistic work with unbelievers: 'testifying (διαμαρτυρόμενος) to the good news of God's grace'; 'preaching (κηρύσσων) the kingdom'; and 'proclaiming (ἀναγγεῖλαι) the whole will of God'. This pattern of instruction was accompanied by his personal warning (νουθετῶν) to individuals 'night and day with tears.' Significantly, however, Paul also expounded the gospel and its implications to the Ephesian Christians, based on the assumption that 'the word of (God's) grace' would build them up (οἰκοδομῆσαι), and give them 'an inheritance among all those who are sanctified' (20:32).

Paul's pastoral peaching was a continuing exposition of the gospel and its implications, set within the framework of biblical teaching about the kingdom of God and the overall purpose or plan of God.

Presumably, he did this with reference to Old Testament Scripture, as witnessed by a number of his letters. Indeed, it is the pattern of his letters more than any sermon in Acts that illustrates the sort of teaching he gave to Christian congregations.

3.1.2. A charge to Timothy

In 1 Timothy 4:13, Paul urges his younger colleague to devote himself 'to the public reading of Scripture, to preaching and to teaching.' This was to be the regular pattern of his ministry in the same Ephesian church that Paul addressed. The word translated 'preaching' by the *NIV* is παράκλησις, which is more literally rendered 'exhortation' by *ESV*, *HCSB*. The sequence in this verse suggests that the reading aloud of Scripture was accompanied by an address that explained the meaning and significance of the text, and urged God's people to respond to its implications. We often equate the preacher with the teacher, but what is the role of exhortation in biblical preaching? Do we give enough space and attention to this ministry?

It is worth noting the way the New Testament employs παράκλησις and related terms. Depending on the context, it refers to comfort, encouragement, exhortation, persuasion, or admonition.[1] The terminology is widely used for a range of public and private ministries (e.g., Acts 2:40; 11:23; 14:22; 15:32; 16:40; 20:1-3). This prophetic-type activity applies revealed truth to the needs and situation of a particular individual or group of people. Some biblical texts lend themselves more obviously to exhortation in a positive sense, others to warning. But there is value in reflecting on the 'paraklētic' implications of every passage.

3.1.3. The Ephesian letter

The first three chapters of Paul's letter to the Ephesians are doctrinal, expounding the great truths of the gospel and the plan of God for humanity. The second three chapters are hortatory, arising from the doctrinal exposition. If Paul's charge to Timothy is to combine teaching and exhortation, preachers need to show how the doctrinal passages lead to application, and when the hortatory sections are being expounded the aim will be to ground them in the earlier chapters.

In fact, the mode of Paul's exposition in Ephesians 1-3 points to the way in which we are to receive this teaching and apply it. The praise

---

[1] Cf. O Schmitz, 'παρακαλέω, παράκλησις,' in *Theological Dictionary of the New Testament*, G Kittel & G Friedrich (eds), G W Bromiley (trans.), Vol 5; (Grand Rapids: Eerdmans, 1967); http://davidgpeterson.com/other-topics/ministry-of-encouragement.

format in 1:4-14 is an encouragement to join Paul in praising God for the spiritual blessings he has given us in Christ. The thanksgiving and prayer report in 1:15-23 challenges us to give thanks and pray for one another as Paul does. The celebration of God's redemptive achievement in 2:1-10 and 2:11-21 invites us to question 'how then should we live?' Paul's declaration of his own part in God's plan leads to explicit words of application (3:1-13), and the implied challenge to share again with the apostle in his prayer and praise (3:14-21).

So application is not always a moral imperative or a set of guidelines about living more effectively as a Christian. Preachers must ask why the material they are expounding has been written in the form in which they find it, and think about its rhetorical implications. Hortatory material will only have its intended impact when it is understood in the light of the writer's unfolding of gospel truths.

3.1.4. Pastoral preaching

Taking his cue from Ephesians 4:11-13, Peter Adam concludes that pastoral preaching is 'the *explanation* and *application* of the Word in the assembled congregation of Christ, in order to produce corporate preparation for service, unity of faith, growth, and upbuilding.'[2]

Adam's definition picks up some of the emphases we have noted already, stressing that pastoral preaching is a *public* presentation of *revealed truth* to a *Christian congregation* for their *edification* as a body and *equipment for ministry*. 'This means that the sermon's focus of address is most appropriately not individuals and their needs, but the needs of the congregation as a whole.'[3]

Such a focus is consistent with the nature of most of the biblical books, which were addressed to the people of God collectively in one place or another. Working out the purpose of biblical books within the canon of Scripture is an essential preliminary to expounding them. Adam goes on to detail other ministries of the word that should take place in the life of a congregation, but stresses the importance of what he calls 'the formal monologue' of the sermon. This provides a unique opportunity for the pastor to minister to the gathered church as a local manifestation of the body of Christ.

---

2 Peter Adam, *Speaking God's Words: a Practical Theology of Preaching* (Leicester: Inter-Varsity, 1996), p 71 (my emphasis). He takes 'the Word' in this context to mean the gospel.

3 Adam, *Speaking God's Words*, p 70. Adam (pp 71-72) comments on the danger of public preaching without an accompanying personal ministry to believers by the pastor.

3.2. *Teaching the Bible with pastoral relevance*

3.2.1. *The relevance of systematic expository preaching*

In *The Sermon Under Attack,* Klaas Runia argues that the secret of relevant preaching is that

> the message of the gospel and the situation of the listeners are related to each other in such a way that the listeners discover that its message really concerns their life as it is. *Relevance occurs at the intersection* of the *unique message of the Bible* ... and the *unique situation of the people* in the pew.[4]

Different styles of biblical preaching are possible, including *textual* (where a single verse may be explained and applied), or *topical* (where a doctrinal theme or ethical subject may be examined), or *apologetic* (where a significant objection to biblical teaching is examined and justified). But systematic exposition of biblical passages has the distinct advantage of unfolding biblical revelation in the form that it was given to us. Moreover, this method enables the preacher to teach appropriate ways of handling different biblical genres, and to be guided by the emphases and aims of the biblical writers themselves.

Systematic expository preaching is often criticized because sermons are too dry, too taken up with exegetical detail, and not well applied. Such criticisms say more about the practitioners than about the method itself! But the warnings are apposite. Haddon Robinson advocates a method that leaves room for the Holy Spirit to work through the preacher in bringing about effective communication of revealed truth to a Christian congregation:

> Expository preaching is the communication of a biblical concept, derived from and transmitted through a historical, grammatical and literary study of a passage in its context, which the Holy Spirit *first applies to the personality and experience of the preacher, then through the preacher, applies to the hearers.*[5]

---

4 Klaas Runia, *The Sermon Under Attack* (Exeter: Paternoster, 1983), p75 (author's emphasis).

5 Haddon W Robinson, *Biblical Preaching: The Development and Delivery of Expository Messages* (2nd ed., Grand Rapids: Baker, 1993), p 21 (my emphasis).

Robinson advocates searching for 'the big idea' in a passage.[6] This should take the preacher to the theological heart of the unit, and expose the writer's intention in presenting the material in the form that we have it. With the big idea in mind, the preacher should be able to structure a sermon that draws out the salient points in the passage, and progressively draws the hearers to hear and respond to its central concern. This approach allows for simplicity and profundity at the same time, giving sufficient time to develop and apply the key issue in the passage.

A biblical sermon should not simply be an exegetical study of a passage, but a 'word of exhortation' (Acts 13:15; Hebrews 13:22) that applies the message of Scripture to the life-situation of those addressed. This is what I have called the 'paraklētic' approach. As Robinson argues, this method will be most effective when the Holy Spirit first applies the message to the personality and experience of the preacher, and then through the preacher to the hearers. More will be said about this method below.

3.2.2. Determining appropriate passages and structures for exposition

Dividing books for exposition

Commentaries and lectures on biblical books often divide the material into large sections, broadly based on content or rhetorical style. Sometimes preachers follow these divisions and attempt to cover long chapters or even multiple chapters in a single sermon. It is often argued that this is necessary if a book like Isaiah or Acts is to be covered in a year of preaching. But this practice exposes three questionable assumptions: first, that a whole biblical book needs to be expounded in the shortest time possible, second, that justice can be done to large passages in the space of 25 or 30 minutes, and third, that congregational members will grasp what is being said, and will truly benefit from this approach.

My experience is that you have to be a very gifted expositor and able communicator to carry this off. Sermons that bite off more Scripture than even the preacher can chew tend to be weak on application, and leave congregational members with a degree of biblical indigestion. Whenever young preachers tell me they have been asked to preach on

---

6 Robinson, *Biblical Preaching*, pp 33-46. This means that an expository sermon should convey one major idea, which is the theme of the portion of Scripture on which it is based. This is a good rule of thumb, though there are occasions when the text demands a more complex approach.

large chunks of Scripture, I advise them to choose a section of the appointed passage, and to do their best with that. It is more helpful for preachers and their hearers if a large book is divided into smaller units and the exposition is spread over a longer period of time, perhaps alternating with other sermon series.

Structuring the exposition

Even when a satisfactory division of a biblical book has been made, there is still the issue of discerning the structure and emphases of chosen units. Here the genre and purpose of the particular text ought to be considered. So a narrative or speech may be best handled by highlighting key themes. A psalm may demand that you engage the congregation with the different stages in the experience and mood of the psalmist. A parable may suggest that you look at one or two obvious features of the story and illustrate their significance. Apocalyptic literature may require you to work with larger units, guided by the symbolism and its function in the unfolding structure of the book.[7]

A meaningful homiletical structure can often be derived from the syntactical analysis of a biblical passage, especially when expounding New Testament letters.[8] But it is helpful to keep in mind the goal of exposing 'the big idea' of the unit and relate the different sections of the passage to its central theme. So, for example, we might conclude that the big idea in Romans 5:1-11 is that we should live as those who have been reconciled to God. This theme is introduced in vv. 1-2 in terms of having peace with God, and the passage concludes with explicit claims about being reconciled to God in vv. 10-11. Reconciliation is an important gospel notion, though it is only mentioned in Romans here and in 11:15. So the expository preacher will want to give due time to explaining and applying this theme.

But Paul goes on to link peace with God and 'the hope of the glory of God.' This immediately raises the subject of suffering and how that affects our hope. Paul affirms that 'hope does not put us to shame because God's love has been poured out into our hearts through the Holy Spirit, who has been given to us' (v. 5). Having raised the subject of God's love, the apostle feels bound to focus on the historic expression

---

7 Jeffrey D Arthurs, *Preaching with Variety: How to Recreate the Dynamics of Biblical Genres* (Grand Rapids: Kregel, 2007), suggests different ways of preaching on the different types of literature found in the Bible.

8 Cf. Walter C Kaiser, *Toward an Exegetical Theology: Biblical Exegesis for Preaching and Teaching* (Grand Rapids: Baker, 1981), pp 149-81.

of that love in the death of Christ (vv. 6-8). This then leads the argument back to justification by faith, reconciliation, and the hope of eternal life (vv. 9-11).

So this passage faces the preacher with a challenge: how much will the sermon dwell on the related issues and how much on explaining the controlling idea of peace with God or reconciliation? If the sermon is part of a series, the theme of coping with suffering as we wait to share in the glory of God could be left until 8:18-30 is examined. Similarly, the work of the Holy Spirit in the life of the believer could be mentioned briefly in connection with 5:5, but taken up in detail when 8:1-17 is expounded.

It takes a long time to acquire the necessary skills for relevant expository preaching, and we all need to keep developing in this area. Ministry teams in churches ought to spend time regularly coaching each other in these matters, asking whether too much was attempted in a given sermon, whether the big idea was adequately revealed, whether the genre and structure of the passage was properly exposed, and whether the message was consistently and relevantly applied. Senior ministers should spend time with new preachers, commenting on sermon outlines in advance, and helping them review every aspect of their content and delivery after the event. Constant practice with feedback is the best way to develop good preaching.

3.2.3. Relating the message of biblical passages to the situation of contemporary hearers

Theological analysis

Simplistic application is ruled out by a serious approach to biblical interpretation. In particular, the discipline of Biblical Theology encourages us to look for the salvation-historical and Christological significance of texts. But too often we find ourselves unable to move beyond this level of understanding to the more personal or congregational implications of a text. This is particularly so when we seek to expound the Old Testament.[9]

Theological analysis is critical in the move from exegesis to application. We live in vastly different contexts in the world today, and each of those contexts differs from the particular contexts addressed by

---

9 Graeme L Goldsworthy, *Preaching the Whole Bible as Christian Scripture: The Application of Biblical Theology to Expository Preaching* (Leicester: Intervarsity, 2000) is a helpful guide in this connection.

the biblical books. But God remains the same, and his method of dealing with his people remains the same. So the knowledge of God and his ways that can be discerned from a biblical passage provides us with a key to effective application.

Take, for example, the story of the announcement of the birth of Jesus and Mary's response in Luke 1:26-56. There are profound theological themes here: the faithfulness of God in keeping his promises, the significance of Jesus in the plan and purpose of God, and the extraordinary nature of his conception. But the narrative also focuses on Mary's faith, both with respect to the fulfilment of God's promises, and her own testing role as an unmarried mother. The uniqueness of Mary's situation should not blind us to the hortatory significance of the passage. At the same time, we cannot simply say 'your faith should be like Mary's faith.' Her faith should be understood in terms of the specific encouragements and challenges she received.

Understanding people

Whenever I have felt that my preaching was losing touch, I have been convicted of the need to spend more time with the people I am seeking to pastor. My own discipline has been to try and do the exegetical work as early as possible in the week, and then allow several days for reflection on how the passage affects me personally, and how it will challenge or encourage the people I plan to address.

In full-time pastoral ministry, I found that contacts with members of the congregation during the week, or opportunities to talk to unbelievers, gave me insights about how to preach the text on Sunday. What I was considering in my study went with me into every pastoral engagement. Sometimes I shared aspects of the sermon with individuals to gauge their response, and take account of their questions. These conversations then informed the way I presented the message on Sunday. Being an occasional, itinerant preacher is much more difficult!

Of course, my understanding of people has not been restricted to personal encounters, but has grown through reading novels, newspapers, and magazines, and through watching movies, and television programs. I am always particularly keen to notice what is said about the great issues mentioned in the Bible, even if the people themselves have no explicitly religious disposition. The characters I have met in this way have become conversation partners in some of my sermons!

3.3. *Holistic application*

Some would argue that if the Bible is properly expounded, it will speak directly to believers, and the Holy Spirit will simply apply the message to individual hearts and lives. Some even go so far as suggesting that personal illustrations, memorable stories, or rhetorical techniques can actually hinder the impact of the word. Topical or thematic outlines may obscure the true meaning of a text.

Another line of argument suggests that personal application produces narrowly pietistic preaching. It trivialises the exposition of narratives and prophecy, and avoids the Christ-centred, redemptive-historical meaning of texts. At the other extreme, there are those who contend that only socio-political or ecclesial applications are relevant or appropriate.[10]

If application is a holistic, theological, and pastoral task, it will take account of these concerns, and be truly driven by the biblical text. It will also take account of the situation and spiritual condition of those addressed. Appropriate application involves theological reflection, pastoral wisdom, and communicative skill. It is an aspect of the ministry of comfort, encouragement, exhortation, persuasion, or admonition that I mentioned before. So Peter Adam argues that the ministry of the Word includes 'not only an intellectual or conceptual explanation of the content of the message, but also practical instructions about its impact on the hearers or readers, and an emotional appeal to respond in a certain way.'[11]

3.3.1. *A life-changing aim*

Chris Green reminds us that 'the proper purpose of the Bible is not simply transferring truth about God from him to us, but that through those truths we meet him, know him, love him and obey him.'[12] Considering how preaching can be relevant, he contends that 'it is precisely as we become more biblical that we become more contemporary, and the closer we look at the text, the clearer we see our

---

10 Adam, *Preaching God's Words*, pp 91-120 examines the way different views of Scripture determine the way it is handled in preaching.

11 Adam, *Preaching God's Words*, p 131.

12 Christopher Green, *Cutting to the Heart: Applying the Bible in Preaching and Teaching* (Nottingham: IVP, 2015), p 98 (emphasis removed).

world.'[13] Green's aim is to discover from the Bible itself how we might apply its multi-faceted message.

Murray Capill similarly contends that 'effective expository preaching takes place when biblical faithfulness and insightful application are inextricably bound together. One is neither substituted for, nor overshadowed by, the other.'[14] The sermon is not a lecture or simply an exegetical examination of the text with some applicatory thoughts attached: 'it is, rather, a proclamation today of the meaning of the text for God's people here and now.'[15] The goal of biblical exposition is that people should hear God speak in a life-shaping way in their current situation.

Capill agrees with Jay Adams that 'to apply' in everyday English means 'to bring one thing in contact with another in such a way that the two adhere, so that what is applied *to* something affects that to which it is applied.'[16] Just as we apply paper or paint to a wall, so preachers may take biblical truth and 'press it against or put it on the lives of people.'[17] The ability to do this comes from adequate time spent reflecting on the meaning and significance of the chosen passage for those who are to be addressed. Poorly applied sermons betray a lack of reflection on the unique message of the passage and its intersection with the situation of the listeners.

3.3.2. Heart penetration

Capill is concerned with 'bringing the message as a whole, to the person as a whole, for life as a whole.'[18] The entire message from start to finish should have an applicatory thrust, rather than a few bolt-on suggestions being added at the end! The message should be addressed to the mind, the will, and the emotions, all of which are embraced by the biblical concept of the heart. This engagement should begin as the sermon is introduced, and its relevance is signalled.

Different dimensions of the heart

The New Testament makes it clear that the renewing of *minds* should be our primary concern in ministering to people (e.g. Romans 12:2;

---

[13] Green, *Cutting to the Heart*, pp 150-51 (emphasis removed).

[14] Murray Capill, *The Heart is the Target: Preaching Practical Application from Every Text* (Phillipsburg: P & R, 2014), p 14.

[15] Capill, *The Heart is the Target*, p 17.

[16] Jay Adams, *Truth Applied: Application in Preaching* (Grand Rapids: Ministry Resources Library, 1990), p 15.

[17] Capill, *The Heart is the Target*, p 30.

[18] Capill, *The Heart is the Target*, p 25.

1 Corinthians 14:14-19; Colossians 3:2; Philippians 4:8). Changing the way people think is clearly the 'entrance point to the other faculties of the heart.'[19] *Consciences* may need to be specifically addressed because they are corrupted or 'seared' (Titus 1:15; 1 Timothy 4:1-2), and in need of convicting or guiding (Romans 14:1-23; 1 John 3:19-20). But consciences can also be burdened by guilt, and in need of cleansing from sin (Hebrews 9:14; 10:2, 22). *Wills* need to be moved (Ephesians 4:17–5:20; James 1:22), and godly *passions* need to be aroused (Romans 12:9-16). Capill recommends a top-down approach, ministering to the mind first, but this may be a little restrictive (e.g., in Romans 9 Paul begins with his passion for unbelieving Israelites, and then moves to a scriptural analysis of their situation).

Presenting biblical truth in a heart-penetrating way involves more than selecting appropriate illustrations. The truth of a text, with its disturbing sting or calming assurance, should be *felt* by those who are addressed. The way a story is told or an argument is presented should be reflected in the delivery. So the anguish of David as he acknowledges his transgressions in Psalm 51, and seeks God's transforming grace, should move people to be similarly honest, and express repentance and dependence on God in Christ. The brutal honesty of Ecclesiastes needs to be pressed home to contemporary Christians, as the Teacher begins to evaluate his experience of this life, and considers how to find meaning in worldly pursuits.

Dialoguing with text and audience

Sometimes the biblical text can be dramatized, as you put yourself or the congregation in the position of characters in the passage. Alternatively, you can ask questions of the text, or debate with the author as you go along. You might ask the congregation how they feel or react to what is being communicated. Present the paradoxes of the text in an arresting way, and then seek to resolve them. Keep your listeners actively involved in the learning process by the way you present the issues. This means dialoguing with the congregation as well as with the text, though you may not explicitly ask for verbal responses from your audience. Like Paul in Romans, you could be debating with a hypothetical objector or an honest inquirer, a believer with false confidence, or someone in need of assurance.[20]

---

19 Cf. Capill, *The Heart is the Target*, p 105.

20 Runia, *The Sermon Under Attack*, pp 91-96 offers some helpful guidelines for establishing a dialogue between the text and the hearers.

Prayerful and receptive listeners

Biblical passages should be exposed in a way that challenges attitudes, mind-set, motivations, aspirations, character, and goals. However, Capill argues that 'such holistic, applicatory preaching never stands alone, but is dependent on the presence and power of the Holy Spirit, the fervent prayers of God's people, and the support and reinforcement of a spiritually dynamic church community.'[21]

In other words, congregations should be taught to expect that God will minister to them through the regular exposition of the Bible, and be ready to respond. They need to understand that their *prayers* and *receptivity* are an essential part of the communication process. Train your people to be godly listeners, and feed them with nourishing spiritual food so that they desire more and more of it (cf. Hebrews 5:11-14; 1 Peter 2:2-3)!

3.3.3. A living process

Returning to the point made by Haddon Robinson, we may describe the preaching process in terms of the living word of God addressing the situation of the hearers through the person of the preacher. In the language of communication theory, a meaningful sermon moves from *source* (the biblical text), through *medium* (the preacher), to *recipients* (the congregation). Capill rightly affirms that 'the preacher's life is the laboratory in which biblical truth is tested. Preachers must live the application before they can make it live in the lives of others.'[22]

Listening to Scripture ourselves

Many who have written about biblical preaching begin by considering the impact that Scripture should have on the preacher. Our primary goal is not to work on the text, but *to let the text work on us*. Scripture must have a transforming effect in the lives of those who would expound the Bible, before they can effectively minister God's truth to others.

This is the primary meaning of the well-known claim in 2 Timothy 3:16 that all God-breathed Scripture is 'useful for teaching, rebuking, correcting, and training in righteousness, so that *the servant of*

---

[21] Capill, *The Heart is the Target*, p 45.
[22] Capill, *The Heart is the Target*, p 54. Cf. Timothy Keller, 'A Model for Preaching (Part One),' *Journal of Biblical Counseling* 12, no. 3 (1994), p 36.

God may be thoroughly equipped for every good work.'[23] Timothy is 'the servant of God' who needs to be equipped for his preaching ministry.

But 2 Timothy 3:16, and texts like Romans 15:4 or Hebrews 4:12-13, can also help the preacher discern the aim of a passage for preaching. Is it concerned to teach the truth and rebuke false teaching? Perhaps its aim is to train believers in godly living, and correct wrong patterns of behaviour. More specifically, its intention might be to test the state of people's hearts, and bring conviction of sin. Alternatively, it might seek to encourage and exhort God's people in particular ways.[24]

Drawing on our own experience

If preachers engage with the text personally, they can draw upon the reservoir of their experience in applying it to others. But this does not mean that sermons should be filled with copious illustrations from our own lives.

Capill points to the fact that 'all the preacher has read, learned, thought about, observed, suffered, processed, and experienced has the potential to form a rich reservoir out of which much powerful preaching and penetrating application can flow.'[25] The biblical text should be the primary source of input for every expository sermon, but the life of the preacher is a second source of input. This personal reservoir is filled by our own walk with God, by experiencing life richly with gratitude to God, by learning to be close observers of life in others, and through our knowledge of theology, church, and culture.

3.4. *Getting it across*

3.4.1. *Using illustrations*

Chris Green challenges the practice of looking for timeless truths in the Bible, and highlights the need to take its developing storyline seriously. This involves identifying typological or biblical-theological patterns in the text. However, against those who argue that character studies of any kind are inappropriate, he discerns from the New Testament itself legitimate ways of using biblical characters as examples for Christians.

---

[23] *NIV* 2011 ('the servant of God') is an attempt to convey the specific reference to Timothy and other ministers of the gospel implied by the original ('man of God').

[24] Green, *Cutting to the Heart*, pp 264-78, 312-429, offers numerous examples to help us move from text to application.

[25] Capill, *The Heart is the Target*, p 81.

'We make the exemplary lessons trivial when we take them out of their biblical-theological place; but put them back in, even if it is quite a light context, and they are valid.'[26] To make his point, he focuses on the portrait of Abraham in Romans 4, and draws attention to the biblical cameos in Hebrews 11, and elsewhere.

In my experience, sermon illustrations fall into two categories: they may *clarify the meaning of the biblical text*, or they may *demonstrate ways in which its message may be applied*. An example of the first type might be a comparison of adoption in the contemporary world with what Paul says in Romans 8:14-17 about adoption into the family of God. But this may not take you to the heart of Paul's concern. The passage aims to encourage believers about the Spirit's work, enabling us to call God '*Abba*, Father', and giving us confidence to suffer with Christ in order to be glorified with him. Another illustration is necessary to show how such prayer might be expressed and help us in our discipleship.

3.4.2. *Nine arrows for effective application*

Capill points out that 'explaining the truth doesn't necessarily mean people will accept it, and commanding response doesn't necessarily mean people will do it.'[27] He goes on to describe 'nine arrows' that preachers can use with good effect in impressing biblical truth on people's hearts.

- We can appeal to people's consciences or judgment about an issue
- We can anticipate and answer objections as we engage with the text
- We can give reasons, motivations, and incentives from the text for responding to its message
- We can be culturally specific, pointed, and direct in relating the message to the hearers
- We can use illustrations for both clarity (explaining the text) and impact (showing how we should respond);
- We can provide testimonies to the truth personally or using the experience of others
- We can use testimonies to show what it looks like in practice to respond to the text

---

26 Green, *Cutting to the Heart*, pp 285-309.
27 Capill, *The Heart is the Target*, p 152.

- We can use fresh, vivid words to convey biblical truth
- We can speak personally and passionately from the heart, in order to affect the hearts of others.[28]

3.5. *Conclusion*

Effective pastoral preaching takes place when we give ourselves enough time to reflect on the significance of biblical passages for the people in our care. The impact of a passage on your own life is an important channel for discerning its relevance to others. Getting regular feedback is a way of discovering the helpfulness of your approach to different biblical genres and modes of communication.

The biblical model is to combine instruction and application in the form of comfort, encouragement, exhortation, persuasion, or admonition. This may involve the use of illustrations or testimonies, dialoguing with an imaginary opponent, or facing the congregation with serious questions about their own lives. We should have no doubts about the relevance of the Bible for contemporary Christians, but the challenge for preachers is to expose that relevance each time they stand to deliver its message.

3.6. *Bibliography*

P Adam, *Speaking God's Words: a Practical Theology of Preaching* (Leicester: Inter-Varsity, 1996)

J Adams, *Truth Applied: Application in Preaching* (Grand Rapids: Ministry Resources Library, 1990)

J D Arthurs, *Preaching with Variety: How to Recreate the Dynamics of Biblical Genres* (Grand Rapids: Kregel, 2007)

M Capill, *The Heart is the Target: Preaching Practical Application from Every Text* (Phillipsburg: P & R, 2014)

G L Goldsworthy, *Preaching the Whole Bible as Christian Scripture: The Application of Biblical Theology to Expository Preaching* (Leicester: Intervarsity, 2000)

C Green, *Cutting to the Heart: Applying the Bible in Preaching and Teaching* (Nottingham: IVP, 2015)

W C Kaiser, *Toward an Exegetical Theology: Biblical Exegesis for Preaching and Teaching* (Grand Rapids: Baker, 1981)

[28] Capill, *The Heart is the Target*, pp 166-69 shows how Paul uses seven of these arrows in arguing his case in Romans 9.

T Keller, 'A Model for Preaching (Part One),' *Journal of Biblical Counseling* 12, no. 3 (1994)

H W Robinson, *Biblical Preaching: The Development and Delivery of Expository Messages* (2nd ed., Grand Rapids: Baker, 1993)

K Runia, *The Sermon Under Attack* (Exeter: Paternoster, 1983)

O Schmitz, 'παρακαλέω, παράκλησις,' in *Theological Dictionary of the New Testament*, G Kittel & G Friedrich (eds), G W Bromiley (trans.), Vol 5; (Grand Rapids: Eerdmans, 1967)

4. The Comfort of God and Pastoral Ministry: An Exegetical Study of 2 Corinthians 1:3-7 – *Peter Orr*

4.1. *Introduction: Metaphors for Pastoral Ministry: The Pastor as Therapist*

In their recent book *The Pastor as Public Theologian,*[1] Kevin Vanhoozer and Owen Strachan discuss different metaphors that shape the way pastors think about themselves and their task:

> Metaphors pastors minister by often gain such a grip on the imagination that it sometimes becomes difficult to dislodge them. Such metaphors become pictures that hold us captive. These pictures often reveal more about the concerns of the age in which they were produced than they do about pastors themselves. Indeed, the prevailing picture of the pastor almost always reflects the broader intellectual and cultural influences of the day.[2]

Vanhoozer and Strachan discuss some of the dominant metaphors: the pastor as CEO; as political agitator; as life-coach; as agent of hope and as midwife. One 'especially powerful metaphor' for the pastor's role is that of 'therapist': 'someone who addresses personal and interpersonal problems and effects healing'.[3] Vanhoozer and Strachan suggest that viewing pastoral ministry through this lens can lead to the temptation to so rely on clinical psychology as a discipline in order to appear 'professional' that, as a result, clergy effectively cede authority to other disciplines to control how they think about helping people. As a result, one can no longer 'apply theological categories to personal problems'.[4] So, to take an example, pastors will not primarily (if even at all) think of gluttony and greed as a problem of sin, but as 'symptoms of some underlying psychological or social condition'.[5]

---

1 Kevin J Vanhoozer and Owen Strachan, *The Pastor as Public Theologian: Reclaiming a Lost Vision* (Grand Rapids: Baker Academic, 2015).
2 Vanhoozer and Strachan, *The Pastor as Public Theologian*, p 7.
3 Vanhoozer and Strachan, *The Pastor as Public Theologian*, p 9.
4 Vanhoozer and Strachan, *The Pastor as Public Theologian*, p 10.
5 Vanhoozer and Strachan, *The Pastor as Public Theologian*, p 8.

Andrew Purves[6] has traced the origins of this move in pastoral ministry to Seward Hiltner's 1958 volume *Preface to Pastoral Theology*.[7] Although Hiltner's call for pastoral ministry to draw on the fields of psychology and sociology has its benefits (to paraphrase the apostle Paul: psychological training is of some value), Purves suggests it has had two negative consequences: Firstly, it has cut pastoral theology off from the central Christian doctrines of Christology, Soteriology and the Trinity. Secondly, as a result of the lack of doctrinal foundation, pastoral work has tended 'to be given over to control by secular goals and techniques of care'.[8] In his volume, Purves proposes a 'complete change of direction with regard to pastoral theology' because so 'much pastoral theology seems to be developed without explicit regard for the biblical and doctrinal heritage of Christian confession and so has almost nothing to say as theology'.[9] Pastoral theology, as such, has largely abandoned the responsibility to speak concerning God.

Andrew Purves' volume is a profoundly helpful doctrinal correction to much contemporary pastoral theology. In this chapter, I want, in a very small way, to add to this discussion from a more exegetical point of view. Purves' book is not unconcerned with exegesis, but it is more of a re-calibration of pastoral theology along a doctrinal axis. In this chapter, I would like to offer an exegetical analysis of one passage (2 Corinthians 1:1-7) which highlights one dimension of pastoral ministry. And this passage is particularly relevant because one of its dominant motifs is an image that is very much at home in the world of therapy: *comfort*.

4.2. *Translating 'Comfort'* (παρακαλέῶ παράκλησις)

The language of comfort is found in this passage in nominal (παράκλησις) and verbal (παρακαλέω) forms. There seem to be three

6 Andrew Purves, *Reconstructing Pastoral Theology: A Christological Foundation* (Louisville: Westminster John Knox, 2004).

7 Seward Hiltner, *Preface to Pastoral Theology* (New York: Abingdon, 1958).

8 Purves, *Reconstructing Pastoral Theology*, p xiv.

9 Purves, *Reconstructing Pastoral Theology*, p xvii.

main senses of the verb παρακαλέω: to urge; to plead and to comfort.[10] Interestingly, in different parts of the Bible different meanings tend to dominate.

4.2.1. *The Old Testament*

In the Old Testament the sense of 'comfort' dominates. That is, the Greek verb παρακαλέω tends to render the Hebrew נחם which has the meaning 'to comfort' and is often used in contexts of grief:

- Genesis 24:67 'Then Isaac brought her into the tent of Sarah his mother and took Rebekah, and she became his wife, and he loved her. So Isaac was *comforted* after his mother's death.'[11]
- Isaiah 51:3 'For the LORD *comforts* Zion; he *comforts* all her waste places and makes her wilderness like Eden, her desert like the garden of the LORD; joy and gladness will be found in her, thanksgiving and the voice of song.'
- 1 Chronicles 7:22 'And Ephraim their father mourned many days, and his brothers came to *comfort* him.'

4.2.2. *The Gospels*

In the Gospels, the verb is most frequently used of people imploring or pleading with Jesus:

- Matthew 8:5-6 'When he entered Capernaum, a centurion came forward to him, *appealing* to him, "Lord, my servant is lying paralyzed at home, suffering terribly".'
- Mark 1:40 'And a leper came to him, *imploring* him, and kneeling said to him, "If you will, you can make me clean".'
- Luke 8:31 'And they *begged* him not to command them to depart into the abyss.'

However, the notion of comfort or consolation is also present:

---

[10] Cf. Walter Bauer *et al.*, *A Greek-English Lexicon of the New Testament and Other Early Christian Literature* (3rd ed; Chicago: University of Chicago Press, 2000), loc. which lists five main options: (1) to ask to come and be present where the speaker is, call to one's side; (2) to urge strongly, appeal to, urge, exhort, encourage; (3) to make a strong request for someth., request, implore, entreat; (4) to instill someone with courage or cheer, comfort, encourage, cheer up (5) treat someone in an inviting or congenial manner, [...] invite in, conciliate, be friendly to or speak to in a friendly manner. (1) is somewhat synonymous with (2) (and (5) is rare).

[11] All English translations in this chapter are from the *ESV* unless otherwise indicated.

- Matthew 5:4 'Blessed are those who mourn, for they shall be *comforted.*'
- Luke 2:25 'Now there was a man in Jerusalem, whose name was Simeon, and this man was righteous and devout, waiting for the *consolation* of Israel, and the Holy Spirit was upon him.'
- Luke 16:25 'But Abraham said, 'Child, remember that you in your lifetime received your good things, and Lazarus in like manner bad things; but now he is *comforted* here, and you are in anguish.'

4.2.3. *Paul*

In Paul's letters, though all 3 senses are present, the meaning 'urge' or 'appeal' or 'exhort' is dominant:

- 1 Corinthians 16:12 'Now concerning our brother Apollos, I strongly *urged* him to visit you with the other brothers, but it was not at all his will to come now. He will come when he has opportunity.'
- Ephesians 4:1 'I therefore, a prisoner for the Lord, *urge* you to walk in a manner worthy of the calling to which you have been called.'
- 1 Thessalonians 4:1 'Finally, then, brothers, we ask and *urge* you in the Lord Jesus, that as you received from us how you ought to walk and to please God, just as you are doing, that you do so more and more.'
- Titus 2:15 'Declare these things; *exhort* and rebuke with all authority. Let no one disregard you.'
- Philemon 10 'I *appeal* to you for my child, Onesimus, whose father I became in my imprisonment.'

4.2.4. *2 Corinthians*

In 2 Corinthians we see examples of each sense of the word:

- 12:8 'Three times I *pleaded* with the Lord about this, that it should leave me.'
- 12:18 'I *urged* Titus to go, and sent the brother with him.'
- 7:6b 'But God, who *comforts* the downcast, *comforted* us by the coming of Titus.'

In fact, this is something of a 2 Corinthians word. Paul himself has over half of the occurrences of παρακαλέω and the cognate noun παράκλησις in the NT and almost half of these are in 2 Corinthians.[12] When we think of the meaning 'exhort', 'urge' or 'appeal' this is to be expected given Paul's somewhat tempestuous relationship with the Corinthians. However, precisely because of this somewhat tense relationship, the notion of παρακαλέω and παράκλησις with the meaning 'comfort' is perhaps a little surprising. The terminology with this sense is concentrated in our focus passage 1:3-7 and in 7:4-13. As we have seen, using παρακαλέω with the sense 'comfort' is not unique to 2 Corinthians, but what Paul does here that he doesn't do elsewhere is have *God* as the subject of the verb παρακαλέω. God is the one who comforts. Even though Paul speaks of himself being able to comfort (1:4) those in affliction, the ultimate origin of this comfort is God. Furthermore, Paul also unpacks a Christological dimension to comfort in 1:5 'as we share abundantly in Christ's sufferings, so *through Christ* we share abundantly in comfort too'. So, it seems that in our passage Paul is developing a theology of comfort. Or, as Hafeman puts it, '[i]f Paul is the apostle of comfort within the New Testament, then 2 Corinthians is the letter of comfort, with 1:3-7 being the paragraph of comfort'.[13]

Also relevant is what we might call the reasons for this comfort. The words for 'affliction' (θλῖψις and the related θλίβω) and 'suffering' (πάθημα) occur more frequently in 2 Corinthians than anywhere else in the NT and more frequently in 1:3-11 than anywhere else in the letter. And so from the very beginning of this letter 'the reader's attention is fixed on the problem of suffering and the promise of God's comfort'.[14]

It is most likely that Paul's theology of 'comfort' has its origins in the OT. The word παρακαλέω is used in a wide range of Graeco-Roman contexts.[15] However, it is used very rarely in what are called the consolatory texts, and in the most famous of these works it doesn't occur at all.[16] Further, in the rare occurrences when it is used, God is

---

[12] In the New Testament there are 109 occurrences of the verb παρακαλέω and 29 of the cognate noun παράκλησις. Of these 138 occurrences of the two words, 74 occur in Paul's letters – and 29 of Paul's uses occur in 2 Corinthians.

[13] Scott Hafemann, *2 Corinthians* (NIVAC 8; Kindle Edition; Grand Rapids: Zondervan, 2000), Kindle Locations 1079-1082.

[14] Scott Hafemann, *2 Corinthians*, pp 1082-1092.

[15] Laura Dawn Alary, 'Good Grief: Paul as Sufferer and Consoler in 2 Corinthians 1:3-7: A Comparative Investigation' (PhD dissertation; University of St Michael's College, Toronto, 2003), p 48.

[16] See Alary, 'Good Grief', p 48 n. 146. These texts are letters or treatises which seek to offer comfort to those who are grieving. An example would be Cicero's *Tusculan Disputations*.

never the subject of the verb παρακαλέω. He is only ever the direct object (i.e. the object of the mourners imploring and beseeching). As such, Paul's understanding of παράκλησις is most likely to be drawn from the OT rather than the Graeco-Roman consolatory tradition.

Can we narrow it down more? Is there one part of the OT that Paul is particularly reflecting on? Where in the OT does God himself offer παράκλησις? The two main clusters are in the Psalms and Isaiah – particularly from chapter 40 onwards.

So, in the Psalms we see the Psalmist call out for comfort from God e.g. Psalm 119 [LXX 118]:76 'Let your steadfast love comfort me according to your promise to your servant'.[17] Although in the Psalms you do have the idea that God has comforted,[18] the dominant idea is the Psalmist *asking* God to bring comfort.[19]

But it is perhaps Isaiah where the note of God as the one who comforts is strongest:

- 51:12 'I, I am he who comforts you (ἐγώ εἰμι ἐγώ εἰμι ὁ παρακαλῶν σε) who are you that you are afraid of man who dies, of the son of man who is made like grass.'
- 57:18 'I have seen his ways, and healed him, and comforted him, and given him true comfort' (παράκλησιν ἀληθινήν).
- 66:13 'As one whom his mother comforts, so I will comfort you.'

In Isaiah, although the comfort of God can actually refer to God's rescue of Israel from exile itself (51:3), it also frequently refers to God's promise of comfort to those who are grieving or mourning. Though they grieve because of the exile, they will be comforted by God ending the exile (40:1-2; 40:11; 41:27; 49:10; 49:13; 51:18-19; 57:18; 61:2; 66:13). That is, the *announcement* of God's rescue itself brings comfort to God's people.

It seems likely that in our passage Paul is drawing on Isaiah and especially Isaiah 40–66. Not only is there widespread agreement that this section of Isaiah shapes much of Paul's letter,[20] Paul also draws a close connection between salvation and comfort (1:6) which echoes

---

17 Cf. also Psalm 22 [LXX 23]:4 ; 71 [70]: 21; 86 [85]: 17; 90 [89]:13; 119 [118]: 50, 52, 82; 135 [134]: 14.

18 E.g. 86 [85]:17.

19 E.g. in 86 [85]:17 the Psalmists calls God to act in line with the comfort he has already given.

20 See, for example, Mark Gignilliat, *Paul and Isaiah's Servants: Paul's Theological Reading of Isaiah 40-66 in 2 Corinthians 5.14-6.10* (LNTS 330; London: T&T Clark, 2007).

Isaiah, especially 40:1-5 where God's comforting words relate to Israel's salvation.

4.2.5. *Translating παρακαλέω and παράκλησις*

When we consult the different English versions, there is near unanimity in rendering παρακαλέω and παράκλησις as 'comfort' in chapter 1 e.g. 1:3-4 'the God of all comfort who comforts us in every affliction'.[21] However, it has been suggested that the English words 'encourage' and 'encouragement' are more appropriate since the idea of comfort can be misunderstood to be 'a languorous feeling of contentment'. 'Encouragement', it is argued, reflects the idea that what Paul has in view 'is not some tranquilizing dose of grace that only dulls pains but a stiffening agent that fortifies one in heart, mind, and soul'.[22] This is a helpful corrective, but as long as we understand 'comfort' correctly, the connections with Isaiah 40–66 are significant enough for us to retain the common translation 'comfort'.

4.3. *An Exegetical Examination of 2 Corinthians 1:3-7*

Verse 3 Blessed be the God and Father of our Lord Jesus Christ, the Father of mercies and God of all comfort

Following his greeting in verses 1 and 2, Paul begins his letter with a benediction rather than his more usual thanksgiving. Some have argued that this is because he had such a low view of the Corinthians that he had nothing to give thanks for![23] However, this idea doesn't fit with the deep love and emotion Paul expresses for the Corinthians throughout the letter. Rather, Paul begins by blessing God to model for the Corinthians from the very beginning a Christian response to suffering.[24] Like 'the psalmist of old, Paul declares God "blessed" because of the consolation he has personally experienced in the midst of affliction'.[25] He makes two parallel descriptions of God: 'the God and Father of our Lord Jesus Christ' and 'the Father of all compassion and

[21] One of the very few that doesn't is the *New American Bible* (not to be confused with the *New American Standard Bible*) which renders the word 'encourage'.

[22] David Garland, *2 Corinthians* (NAC; Nashville: Broadman & Holman, 1999), p 60.

[23] Victor P Furnish, *II Corinthians: A New Translation with Introduction and Commentary* (AB 32A; New York: Double Day, 1984), pp 116-117 cites this as a possibility but rejects it.

[24] So George Guthrie, *2 Corinthians* (BECNT; Grand Rapids: Baker, 2015), p 63.

[25] L L Welborn, 'Paul's Appeal to the Emotions in 2 Corinthians 1:1-2:13; 7:5-16', *JSNT* 82 (2001): 58 cited in Guthrie, *2 Corinthians*, p 65.

the God of all comfort (παρακλήσεως)'. This opening blessing of God has echoes with Psalm 103 [102 LXX] where David blesses the Lord and describes him as the God who crowns him with mercy and compassion (ἐλέει καὶ οἰκτιρμοῖς 103 [102]:4) and like a Father who has mercy on his sons (καθὼς οἰκτίρει πατὴρ υἱούς).[26] In naming God, Paul is following the example of the psalmists who frequently identify him 'in immediate relation to their need or that of Israel'.[27] For example, 'God of my righteousness' (Psalm 4:1); 'God of our salvation' (Psalm 85:4); 'God of vengeance' (Psalm 94:1). In this context he is the God of 'all comfort' suggesting that he offers comfort and encouragement in every circumstance as Paul is about to make clear (1:4).

Verse 4: who comforts us in all our affliction, so that we may be able to comfort those who are in any affliction, with the comfort with which we ourselves are comforted by God.

What does Paul mean by 'affliction' (θλῖψις) here? In Biblical Greek the word is overwhelmingly used of external[28] tribulation and in the immediate context of 1:8 that certainly seems to be the sense, but in a few instances can be used of *internal* distress, and that is certainly the case in 2 Corinthians.[29] In chapter 6:4 he speaks of how he commends himself to them 'by great endurance, in afflictions, hardships, calamities, beatings, imprisonments, riots, labours, sleepless nights, hunger'. He continues 'as sorrowful, yet always rejoicing'. In chapter 11 although Paul does not use the word θλῖψις, he lists the afflictions or troubles that he has experienced: imprisonments, countless beatings, near death experiences, receiving 39 lashes 5 times, being shipwrecked, adrift at sea, constant threat, toil and hardship, hunger and thirst. But he also speaks (11:28) of 'the daily pressure [of his] anxiety for all the churches'. Perhaps most clearly in 7:5 Paul speaks of being afflicted in every way (ἐν παντὶ θλιβόμενοι) and then speaks of 'fightings without and fears within'. Even in the immediate context of our passage he can

---

[26] This parallel noted by Guthrie, *2 Corinthians*, p 67. Paul Barnett, *The Second Epistle to the Corinthians* (NICNT; Grand Rapids: Eerdmans, 1997), p 70 cites a later synagogue prayer (which he argues reflects an earlier tradition): 'May the Lord of consolations comfort you. Blessed be he who comforts the mourners' (Ketubot 8B, 27).

[27] Mark Seifrid, *The Second Letter to the Corinthians* (PNTC; Grand Rapids: Eerdmans, 2015), p 18.

[28] E.g. Exodus 4:31; Deuteronomy 28:53; 1 Samuel 26:24.

[29] E.g. of the distress 'of Joseph's soul' in Genesis 42:21. Possibly Psalm 25[LXX 24]:17. Seifrid, *Second Letter to the Corinthians*, p 23 is perhaps a little harsh to chide the *NIV* for its translation of 'trouble' in 1:4 as being 'not entirely wrong' but being 'weak' given that it 'unfortunately omits the inward experience of trial that *thlipsis* communicates'.

speak of 'despairing of life itself' (1:8). So, in the context of tribulation and affliction as well as external happenings (shipwrecks, beatings etc.), Paul can speak of anxiety, sorrow, fear and despair. Patently, the two are related: external distress produces internal anguish and God is able to comfort the believer in both.

Paul has been comforted by God so that[30] he, in turn, is enabled to comfort those in any affliction. The idea that only those who have suffered were able to help those that suffer was familiar enough in the ancient world. But what differentiates this from a piece of folk wisdom is what Paul says next. It is not simply that because Paul has suffered he can *empathise* with the Corinthians – no, he is able to comfort them through the very same comfort with which[31] he is comforted.

Although 'it would be a mistake to press the notion of mediation too strictly, as though Paul supposed his readers could not themselves receive comfort directly from God',[32] the notion of agency and mediation is clearly present. God comforts Paul and Paul comforts the Corinthians through that same comfort. Does this just apply to Paul or to the Corinthians as well? Paul ends his letter with a call for the Corinthians to comfort one another (13:11). So, comforting is the domain of every Christian. As Harris puts it:

> If v.4 enunciates a universal Christian principle that is applicable to Paul as to all believers, v.5 grounds that principle in specific Pauline experience as a prelude to v.6 with its unambiguous distinction between Corinthian and Pauline experience.[33]

Verse 5 Because just as the sufferings of Christ abound to us, so through Christ our comfort also abounds.

In verse 5 perhaps the shift in language from 'affliction' to 'suffering' 'places even greater emphasis on the *human experience* of pain and sorrow'.[34] But what does Paul mean by the 'sufferings of Christ'? Broadly we can classify suggested interpretations into three groups:[35]

---

30 Understanding the εἰς τὸ δύνασθαι as a purpose clause.

31 The relative pronoun ἧς (which one would expect to be dative as the indirect object of παρακαλέω) is genitive by attraction.

32 M E Thrall, *A Critical and Exegetical Commentary on the Second Epistle to the Corinthians* (ICC; 2 vols; London: T&T Clark, 1994), p 1:104.

33 Murray J Harris, *The Second Epistle to the Corinthians: A Commentary on the Greek Text* (NIGTC; Grand Rapids: Eerdmans, 2005), p 145.

34 Seifrid, *Second Letter to the Corinthians*, p 26.

35 Following Kar Yong Lim, *The Sufferings of Christ are Abundant in Us* (LNTS; London: T&T Clark, 2009), p 45.

(a) messianic woes; (b) mystical union; and (c) imitation of Christ. The most convincing and straightforward option is that of Lim who proposes a narratival interpretation so that Paul understands τὰ παθήματα τοῦ Χριστοῦ as the sufferings [Paul] experienced in his apostolic ministry. It is said to be 'of Christ' because Paul views his suffering of every kind as an expression of the same kind of sufferings Christ experienced in his mission. As such, the genitive τοῦ Χριστοῦ can be seen as a genitive of relationship. As an apostle called by Christ, it is not surprising that Paul would ground the reflection of his sufferings in that of his crucified Lord. As Christ had to suffer persecution and rejection in mission, so Paul is not exempted from suffering in his ministry of the gospel.[36]

So, the 'identification of the suffering of Paul with Christ is best explained in view of the missiological (not ontological) identity between Paul's own suffering as an apostle and the cross of Christ'.[37] In other words, for Paul, 'the sufferings of Christ' perhaps differed from human suffering in general not by their nature but by the person of the sufferer and the purpose of the suffering.[38] It is 'suffering experienced while engaged in [Christ's] service and for the benefit for his church'.[39] As such, Paul can speak of the sufferings of Christ abounding to him and the Corinthians also being participants in that same suffering (v.7).[40]

What does Paul mean when he says 'so through Christ' our comfort abounded? If Christ is the particular reason for Paul's suffering, he is also the means by which God comforts Paul. We see a similar pattern in 12:9-10 where having pleaded (παρεκάλεσα) with the Lord (Jesus) for the removal of the thorn in the flesh, the Lord says to him: 'My grace is sufficient for you, for my power is made perfect in weakness.' As a result Paul reflects as follows:

> Therefore I will boast all the more gladly of my weaknesses, so that the power of Christ may rest upon me. For the sake of Christ (ὑπὲρ Χριστου), then, I am content with weaknesses, insults, hardships, persecutions, and calamities. For when I am weak, then I am strong.

---

36 Lim, *The Sufferings of Christ*, p 52.

37 S Hafemann, 'The Role of Suffering in the Mission of Paul', in *The Mission of the Early Church to Jews and Gentiles*, Jostein Ådna and Hans Kvalbein (eds); (Tübingen: Mohr, 2000), p 174 cited in Lim, *The Sufferings of Christ*, p 52.

38 Harris, *Second Epistle to the Corinthians*, p 146.

39 Harris, *Second Epistle to the Corinthians*, p 146.

40 Harris, *Second Epistle to the Corinthians*, p 146.

Paul is comforted by the Lord's promise of grace. It is the Lord *speaking* to him that comforts and strengthens him to suffer for Christ. This suffering, this affliction that Paul endures and in which he receives comfort is not just for his own sake but for the Corinthians as he makes clear in the following verse.

Verse 6 If we are distressed, it is for your comfort and salvation; if we are comforted, it is for your comfort, which produces in you patient endurance of the same sufferings we suffer.

The Corinthians suffer the same sufferings as Paul. They are the same sufferings not because they are *identical* to Paul's in nature but because they are also the 'sufferings of Christ' which the Corinthians 'endured in union with Christ and for the sake of Christ'.[41] And yet we see a difference between Paul and the Corinthians in that Paul is afflicted and comforted *for the Corinthians.* If he is afflicted it is for *their* comfort. If he is comforted it is for their comfort. There is a mono-directional nature to this comfort and salvation dynamic. Paul is afflicted and comforted *for them.* We will return to the significance of that below, but we also need to note that here Paul connects their comfort and their salvation ('if we are afflicted it is for your comfort *and salvation*'). Without wanting to suggest that comfort and salvation are identical, they are clearly connected. The Corinthians' salvation in some sense depends on their comfort. Comfort, then, is not mere emotional equilibrium. Rather, it is Corinthians being in the state that means that they will persevere and so be saved in the end.

But Paul sees their comfort and salvation as dependent on his own affliction. In what sense can and does Paul's affliction secure their comfort and their salvation? It seems likely that Paul is drawing on the language and theology of Isaiah, particularly Isaiah 40–66. In this section of Isaiah we see this same interplay between God comforting the people and this comfort coming through human mediators:

- 40:11 'He will tend his flock like a shepherd and gather lambs with his arm and comfort those that are with young.'
- 51:12 'I am, I am he who comforts you.' Cf. 41:27; 49:10; 51:3; 57:18.

But you also have verses where comfort is mediated through human agents:

---

[41] Harris, *Second Epistle to the Corinthians,* p 148.

- 35:4 'Comfort those who panic, "Be strong! Do not fear! Look, your God comes to avenge! With divine retribution he comes to deliver you."' [42]

Comfort here, though it originates in God, is mediated through the prophet and the human agents whom he commands. It consists in the proclamation of God's saving activity.[43]

Similarly in Isaiah 61 the prophet describes, in language resonant of the Servant songs, how he has been anointed 'to comfort those who mourn' (61:2). So a dominant note in Isaiah is that God's comfort comes through proclamation by human beings – proclamation of restoration from exile.

This is a pattern repeated throughout the prophets where we see the prophet bringing the word of comfort and consolation to Israel, but where we also see the prophets suffer as they bring that word. The word is continually rejected and so the prophets suffer, but they continue to proclaim the word of comfort. 'To be a prophet,' writes Abraham Heschel, 'is both a distinction and an affliction'.[44]

Whether or not Paul identifies himself as a prophet, his ministry is clearly rooted in the ministry of the prophets and his suffering like that of the prophets is a suffering that results from his proclamation of God's message of comfort.

This connection between comfort and salvation is also indicated in the second half of 2 Corinthians 1:6. But there is a translation issue here which we can see if we compare the *NIV* and the *ESV*:

> *ESV*: 'it is for your comfort, *which you experience* when you patiently endure the same sufferings that we suffer'
>
> *NIV*: 'it is for your comfort, *which produces* in you patient endurance of the same sufferings we suffer'

Is the comfort something they only experience or is it something that is itself effective? The issue turns on how to translate the participle ἐνεργουμένης which could be either middle or passive. In Paul the verb is used 18 times, 7 of those in a form which would be either middle or

---

[42] *NETS* translation: Albert Pietersma and Benjamin G Wright (eds), *A New English Translation of the Septuagint And the Other Greek Translations Traditionally Included Under that Title* (Oxford: OUP, 2007).

[43] Alary, 'Good Grief', p 89.

[44] Abraham Heschel, *The Prophets* (Philadelphia: The Jewish Publication Society of America, 1962), p 9 cited in Alary, 'Good Grief', p 89.

passive. However, in each other case, as Seifrid notes, the middle is employed 'in order to underscore the self-operative nature of the powers he names as the subjects of the verb'.[45] So, it would seem best to understand the comfort here as a dynamic power that produces steadfastness. Comfort produces steadfastness which results in final salvation.

Verse 7 And our hope for you is certain because we know that just as you are participants in sufferings, so you are also participants in comfort.

Paul here reaches the climax of his benediction. His hope for their comfort and salvation (cf. v.6b) is firm, or better, 'guaranteed'[46] because if they suffer they will be comforted. In the following section (1:8-11) Paul is very clear that he wants them to know about his own affliction, God's deliverance of him and the resultant reliance on God that it produced in him. To embrace Paul, to embrace his gospel, is to embrace suffering and affliction.

4.4. *Conclusions*

In this section we will draw some threads together by addressing some questions.

4.4.1. *What exactly does Paul mean by the 'comfort of God'?*

To draw together what we see in this passage: Comfort pertains to any and every affliction – internal and external (v.4); comfort though mediated by Paul ultimately comes from God, the God of all comfort (v.4); comfort can be passed on to others (v.4); comfort is mediated through Christ (v.5); Paul can suffer for their comfort (v.6); Comfort is connected with salvation – it is not simply a feeling of emotional stability; comfort is dynamic in that it produces perseverance in them. In summary, comfort is that which is necessary to enable the person who is afflicted to persevere so that their future salvation is secure.

4.4.2. *In what form does it come?*

The link between comfort and salvation, the fact that Paul can be afflicted for their comfort and the connection between both of these and

---

45 Seifrid, *The Second Epistle to the Corinthians,* p 28 notes Romans 7:5 (the law); 2 Corinthians 4:12 (death); Galatians 5:6 (faith through love); Ephesians 3:20 (power); Colossians 1:29 (God's power); 1 Thessalonians 2:13 (God's word); 2 Thessalonians 2:7 (the mystery of lawlessness).

46 Barnett, *The Second Epistle to the Corinthians,* p 79.

the prophetic literature highlight the fact that this comfort comes centrally through the proclamation of the Word of God. The comfort Paul has in view here is the word of God appropriately spoken to someone who is suffering. Those afflicted are comforted by Paul when they believe the Word he proclaims. And so they can't receive comfort unless they hear the Word – and they can't hear the Word if Paul doesn't speak the Word to them. But, just like the prophets of old, to speak the Word to the Corinthians means affliction and suffering for Paul. There are a number of other passages in 2 Corinthians where this pattern is repeated. Although they don't necessarily use the language of comfort they do speak of what we might broadly say is the restoration or consolation of the Corinthians.

So, in 4:4-13 the themes of proclamation, affliction and restoration (life in this case) are woven together. As Paul is 'afflicted in every way' (4:8) he carries the death of Jesus in his body (4:10) and as he does so, he speaks (4:13). The result is death at work in Paul (4:11) and life is at work in the Corinthians (4:12) and this is all for their sake (4:15). Similarly, in 5:13-21 as Paul suffers ('we are beside ourselves'; 5:13) he speaks from God and the Corinthians are reconciled. Paul describes himself as 'ambassadors for Christ' through whom God 'makes his appeal (παρακαλοῦντος)': 'We implore you on behalf of Christ, be reconciled to God' (5:20). Again, in 6:2-13 Paul speaks and is afflicted for their salvation (6:2 'now is the day of salvation'; 6:4-7 'as servants of God we commend ourselves in every way: by great endurance, in afflictions [...] by truthful speech'; 6:11 'we have spoken freely to you'). In chapters 10-13 Paul underscores that everything he endures is for their edification and restoration (10:8 the Lord has given Paul authority for building them up; 12:19 he has 'been speaking in Christ, and all for your up-building, beloved'; 13:9 'your restoration is what we pray for').

Though the language differs, the theme of 1:3-7, namely their comfort and salvation, is picked up throughout the letter in the different images of restoration, edification, salvation and reconciliation. As Paul proclaims the word of Christ, even in affliction, his goal is their comfort. Paul comforts them as the suffering apostle who proclaims the word of Christ to them.

4.4.3. *What in this passage is unique for Paul as an apostle and what is transferrable to contemporary Christian ministers?*

There are aspects of this passage that apply equally to Paul as to the Corinthians (as Paul comforts them, so they can comfort one another cf. 13:11 'comfort one another' [παρακαλεῖσθε]). So Paul and the Corinthians suffer and are comforted. And both are enabled to offer comfort to others. What is unique for Paul, though, is the number of people for whom he is responsible to comfort. So, in 1:6 Paul's suffering and comfort is for the Corinthians – and presumably for the other churches he had founded and for which he felt anxious (11:29). Thus, it is not the experience of suffering that is unique to Paul with respect to the Corinthians but the extent. Because of his responsibility for the Corinthians and other churches he suffers for a wide group of people.

So, we can cautiously move from Paul to the Christian leader. The Christian leader comforts their flock, their congregation, their Bible study group etc. as they proclaim the word: the word of Christ, the word of salvation, the word of comfort. There is both a positive and negative aspect to this. Positively proclaiming the word of comfort means proclaiming the hope available in Christ. The hope of the resurrection will bring tremendous comfort and salvation.

But true comfort can only come through the whole counsel of God and preaching *this* may involve suffering. It involves teaching the truth even when it is deeply unpopular. The call to repentance, the call to reject the world's values, the unpopular truth about the uniqueness of Christ or the rightness of the Bible's teaching on sexuality. People need to hear these things if they are to be truly comforted, if they are to receive the comfort that will actually produce perseverance in them which will result in final salvation.

In following Paul, the Christian leader will suffer in a more direct, intentional way than the people to whom they are ministering. The apostle was clear that everything he experienced was 'for their benefit' (4:15). The intensity of feeling that the apostle has for the Corinthians comes out at different points in the letter (6:11-12 'We have spoken freely to you, Corinthians, and opened wide our hearts to you. We are not withholding our affection from you'; 7:3 'I have said before that you have such a place in our hearts that we would live or die with you'). As such, Paul's relationship to the Corinthians is the antithesis of the professional minister who stands at a distance from his congregation – only ministering in a detached and distant way from the pulpit.

4.4.4. *What is the function of this passage in the letter?*

It seems on first reading that Paul is writing to comfort them in the midst of the sufferings they were undergoing – to reassure them that God would comfort them. However when we situate this passage in the context of the rest of the letter it is noteworthy that Paul does not refer to any significant persecutions that the Corinthians were undergoing.[47] Are they, in fact, sharing in the sufferings of Christ? If we take 1:6-7 as gnomic descriptions of reality rather than as descriptions of what the Corinthians were actually experiencing, it would fit with the fact that this is a church that across both (extant) letters seems to display a high correspondence with worldly values.

It is precisely the comfort of God that enables the Christian churches to distinguish themselves from the world. It is precisely this which contemporary churches need to hear today. If Christians turn away from the world, they will suffer. Like Paul they will experience the sufferings of Christ. And so they will need the fortitude of the comfort of God through Jesus Christ. It is this comfort which will strengthen them to persevere for final salvation.

2 Corinthians 1:3-7, then, is not in the *first instance* a help to those who are, for example, grieving or experiencing other psychological distress. This passage was written to a church – not to a college of pastors. Its function is to shape the Corinthians' view of the Christian life – to turn them away from the super-apostles who Paul mentions at the end of the letter – men who proclaimed a gospel of victory and glory.

This was not a church that had suffered greatly to this point. The comfort of God would not have been something they currently felt they needed. They were being drawn to the more attractive ministry of the super apostles. As John Barclay has noted (with respect to 1 Corinthians in particular): 'One of the most significant, but least noticed, features of Corinthian church life is the absence of conflict in the relationship between Christians and "outsiders".'[48]

In holding before them the prospect of the comfort of God to meet the sufferings of Christ, the sufferings that he is enduring, Paul is calling them to reorientate their Christian life away from the super-apostles to a suffering apostle who follows a suffering Christ. They need not fear because they will be comforted, they will be sustained. As such 1:7 'And our hope for you is firm, because we know that just as you

47 Thrall, *Second Epistle to the Corinthians*, p 113: 'Perhaps Paul hopes to encourage his readers to imitate his own example of exposure to affliction by writing as though they were already doing so'. She cites Furnish, *II Corinthians*, p 121 who observes that Paul's expressions of confidence of this kind 'are often implicitly hortatory'.

48 John M G Barclay, 'Thessalonica and Corinth: Social Contrasts in Pauline Christianity', *JSNT* 15 (1992), pp 57-8.

share in our sufferings, so also you share in our comfort' is an implicit call to share, to become partners in suffering with Paul.[49]

In practice then this passage applies to the pastor and the Christian leader as they remind the people of the comfort that is available to them. The pastor is to call people to reject the world's view of comfort, and worldly views of Christian ministry. These may result in ease and peace with the world but Jesus came with a sword and to bring division. True Christianity will create conflict with the world and for Christians to face that they need to know that comfort is available. So for pastors, teachers, Christian workers, the primary application of this passage is to call people not to line up with the world, but with the apostle Paul whose ministry meant he shared the sufferings of Christ but who received and offered the very comfort of Christ. The world may hate the authentic Christian and suffering will result, but the God of comfort and compassion will bring comfort through the word about Christ.

4.5. *Bibliography*

L D Alary, 'Good Grief: Paul as Sufferer and Consoler in 2 Corinthians 1:3-7: A Comparative Investigation' (PhD dissertation; University of St Michael's College, Toronto, 2003)

J M G Barclay, 'Thessalonica and Corinth: Social Contrasts in Pauline Christianity', *JSNT* 15 (1992)

P Barnett, *The Second Epistle to the Corinthians* (NICNT; Grand Rapids: Eerdmans,1997)

W Bauer *et al.*, *A Greek-English Lexicon of the New Testament and Other Early Christian Literature* (3rd ed; Chicago: University of Chicago Press, 2000)

D Garland, *2 Corinthians* (NAC; Nashville: Broadman & Holman, 1999)

G Guthrie, *2 Corinthians* (BECNT; Grand Rapids: Baker, 2015)

V P Furnish, *II Corinthians: A New Translation with Introduction and Commentary* (AB 32A; New York: Double Day, 1984)

M Gignilliat, *Paul and Isaiah's Servants: Paul's Theological Reading of Isaiah 40-66 in 2 Corinthians 5.14-6.10* (LNTS 330; London: T&T Clark, 2007)

S Hafemann, *2 Corinthians* (NIVAC 8; Kindle Edition; Grand Rapids: Zondervan, 2000)

———, 'The Role of Suffering in the Mission of Paul', in *The Mission of the Early Church to Jews and Gentiles* Jostein Ådna and Hans Kvalbein(eds); (Tübingen: Mohr, 2000)

[49] P T O'Brien, *Introductory Thanksgivings in the Letters of Paul* (NovTSup 9; Leiden: Brill, 1977), p 256.

M J Harris, *The Second Epistle to the Corinthians: A Commentary on the Greek Text* (NIGTC; Grand Rapids: Eerdmans, 2005)

A Heschel, *The Prophets* (Philadelphia: The Jewish Publication Society of America, 1962)

S Hiltner, *Preface to Pastoral Theology* (New York: Abingdon, 1958)

K Y Lim, *The Sufferings of Christ are Abundant in Us* (LNTS; London: T&T Clark, 2009)

P T O'Brien, *Introductory Thanksgivings in the Letters of Paul* (NovTSup 9; Leiden: Brill, 1977)

A Pietersma and B G Wright (eds), *A New English Translation of the Septuagint And the Other Greek Translations Traditionally Included Under that Title* (Oxford: OUP, 2007)

A Purves, *Reconstructing Pastoral Theology: A Christological Foundation* (Louisville: Westminster John Knox, 2004)

M Seifrid, *The Second Letter to the Corinthians* (PNTC; Grand Rapids: Eerdmans, 2015)

M E Thrall, *A Critical and Exegetical Commentary on the Second Epistle to the Corinthians* (ICC; 2 vols; London: T&T Clark, 1994)

K J Vanhoozer and O Strachan, *The Pastor as Public Theologian: Reclaiming a Lost Vision* (Grand Rapids: Baker Academic, 2015)

L L Welborn, 'Paul's Appeal to the Emotions in 2 Corinthians 1:1-2:13; 7:5-16', *JSNT* 82 (2001)

5. Richard Baxter's portrait of the pastor – *Keith Condie*

5.1. *Introduction – the man Richard Baxter*

> 'O man greatly beloved! The Lord hath revealed his secret things to you, for which many a 1000 soul in England shall rise up and blesse God for you.'[1]

So wrote Thomas Wadsworth, a clergyman in Surrey, to Richard Baxter after finding encouragement in Baxter's writings to take up the task of personal catechising amongst those under his pastoral charge. The key work that had such an impact on Wadsworth, *The Reformed Pastor*, continues in print today. Over the centuries this book has shaped the pastoral practice of many and without doubt the flow-on effects have had an impact upon the lives of many thousands of men and women. The recipients of this benefit may not be aware of what they owe to Baxter; perhaps their thankfulness to God for his labours will only become known after the final triumph of Christ.

Richard Baxter is recognised as one of the great Puritan pastors. Born in 1615, he lived through the dramatic events of seventeenth-century English history – the Civil Wars, the collapse of the monarchy and the institutional Church of England, the Restoration, the Glorious Revolution – before dying in 1691.[2] His spiritual awakening came via the influence of his father and the reading of some Puritan devotional works. He was ordained deacon in 1638 and after working as the master of a school and a curate, in 1641 was invited to become the 'lecturer' or preacher at Kidderminster, Worcestershire. His ministry aroused some tensions, and a little over a year later he left the town. From 1645-1647 he served as a chaplain for Colonel Whalley's forces in the parliamentary army. This experience had a profound impact upon Baxter. He was deeply disturbed by revolutionary and sectarian elements within the New Model Army. Furthermore, he believed that the holiness of life that was so central to Christian living was under threat from antinomian teachings that he thought were gaining traction

---

1 N H Keeble & Geoffrey F Nuttall, *Calendar of the Correspondence of Richard Baxter: Volume I, 1638-1660* (Oxford: Oxford University Press, 1991), p 236.

2 For details of Baxter's life, see N H Keeble, 'Baxter, Richard (1615-1691)', *Oxford Dictionary of National Biography*, (Oxford University Press, 2004); online edn, Jan 2008.

amongst the soldiers. For Baxter, the war was calamitous for the cause of the gospel.[3] In 1647 he returned to Kidderminster, and until 1661 exercised a pastoral ministry in the Puritan mould for which he is most famous. Following the Restoration of the monarchy, Baxter was one of many who, by reason of conscience, was unable to assent to the new Act of Uniformity and thus lost his pastoral charge. But he continued a significant work of pastoral oversight by means of his pen and his tongue, through published works, correspondence, personal converse and occasional preaching.

While *The Reformed Pastor* is Baxter's best-known book, it represents but a small part of his vast literary output. He published approximately 140 treatises concerned both with doctrinal matters and the practical aspects of living out the Christian faith. He also wrote many works that engaged with the doctrinal and ecclesiological controversies of his time. Furthermore, a range of unpublished treatises and approximately 1250 items of correspondence shed further light on the man and his ministry. A decision by a group of nonconformist ministers in 1707 to reprint Baxter's practical works has meant that his reputation has been built upon this aspect of his work. But Baxter himself would have wanted to be just as well known for the theological principles that he espoused – principles that he believed were the drivers of faithful Christian practice.

This noteworthy pastor was also an eccentric man. Baxter's personality was never far beneath the surface of his writings. It might well be possible to label him a hypochondriac: he spent much of his relatively long adult life thinking that he would soon die. He did suffer from ill health and in his autobiography (*Reliquiae Baxterianae*) he reveals details of his flatulency and other digestive problems, his frequent bleeding, and pain from toothaches, headaches and gallstones.[4] This sense of his bodily fragility caused him to highly value time. In a poem he wrote:

> A Life still near to Death, did me possess
> With a deep sense of Time's great preciousness.[5]

Such an attitude certainly enabled the volume of material that issued from his pen. It also caused him to argue that pastors should not marry,

---

3 For details of the impact of the Civil War upon Baxter, see Tim Cooper, *John Owen, Richard Baxter and the Formation of Nonconformity* (Farnham, Surrey: Ashgate, 2011), especially chapter 1.

4 Keeble, 'Baxter, Richard (1615-1691)' *ODNB*. See also Tim Cooper, 'Richard Baxter and his Physicians', *Social History of Medicine* 20 (2007), pp 1-19.

5 Richard Baxter, *Poetical Fragments* (London, 1681), p 38.

since marriage required an investment of time that would distract from ministerial responsibilities. Baxter, however, did not heed his own advice, and at age forty-six married the twenty-five year old Margaret Charlton. It appears to have been a very happy relationship. When Baxter was briefly imprisoned in 1669 for allegedly breaching one of the laws designed to keep nonconformity in check, she willingly accompanied him and 'was never so cheerful a companion as then'; Baxter reported that 'we kept House as contentedly and comfortably as at home'.[6] Baxter's eccentricity was also evident in his intellectual life. He read voraciously and mastered most of the western intellectual tradition. Yet much of what he read he found wanting, and arrived at his own distinctive views on a range of issues.[7]

Irrespective of any quirks of personality, Richard Baxter provides a perspective on the nature of a word-based pastoral ministry that is worthy of careful examination. In this chapter we will consider (1) the context of Baxter's ministry, (2) the principles, priorities and practices of his approach to the pastoral task, (3) critically assess this approach, (4) before concluding with some suggestions as to how Baxter's work might be appropriated today.

5.2. *The context of Baxter's ministry*

Baxter's ministry must be set in the context of the Puritan quest to complete the English Reformation. Puritans believed that something good had happened in the religious life of England in the sixteenth century. In the providence of God, under Henry VIII the church had broken from the control of Rome, had undergone liturgical and theological reform in a protestant direction during the reign of Edward VI, and early in Elizabeth's reign had arrived at a protestant settlement of religion. For the Puritans, however, more was needed. These 'hotter sort of protestants'[8] believed that the English church remained 'but halfly reformed'.[9] Ministers needed to be properly trained to preach the pure word of God. Practices not endorsed in Scripture,

6 Richard Baxter, *Reliquiae Baxterianae* (London, 1696), Part 3, pp 50-51.

7 For example, see below for his unique understanding of the doctrine of justification.

8 Percival Wilburn, *A Checke or Reproofe of M. Howlet's Untimely Screeching* (1581), quoted by Patrick Collinson, *The Elizabethan Puritan Movement* (London: Jonathan Cape, 1967), p 27.

9 William Fuller, 'Booke to the queene', *The Seconde Parte of a Register*, ii. p 52, quoted in Collinson, *Puritan Movement*, p 36.

such as using the sign of the cross in baptism, or the wearing of wedding rings, needed to be discontinued. Further liturgical change was in order, for the authorised Prayer Book remained despoiled with Popish residues. Some Puritans also wanted to change the system of church government, from an Episcopalian form to a Presbyterian system. Moreover, they perceived that a key inadequacy was in the area of church discipline – that no matter what advances had been made doctrinally or liturgically, there was no system in place to preserve the holiness of Christ's church and the communion table was often sullied with unrepentant sinners.

Underlying these calls for change was the core Puritan concern – the necessity for a vibrant spirituality. While historians have wrestled with how best to define Puritanism, perhaps the movement is best understood as a particular mode of piety.[10] The Puritans sought to live for God in every aspect of life with all of their being. They wanted biblical spirituality to mark not just their churches, but their villages and towns, in fact, the whole nation. They wanted England to be a city on a hill, a light to the nations, as an exemplar to the world of what a country wholeheartedly dedicated to God might look like. This meant that discipline in the church involved more than simply excommunicating notorious sinners, but should also function in a positive manner. The goal was to see individuals built up in faith so that they might live in a manner that befits those who belong to God. A series of duties were deemed necessary to accomplish this end. Prayer, meditating on the Bible, communion with other believers, and other such practices were key foci in the ministry of Puritan pastors. Richard Baxter was keenly attuned to this agenda and it is to his approach to the pastoral task that we now turn.

5.3. *Principles, priorities and practices from Baxter's approach to the pastoral task*

5.3.1. *Conversion, not structural change, as the key means to reformation*

From its genesis the Puritan movement had pursued a range of strategies in attempting to nudge the English nation in the direction of true godliness. As noted above, some pushed for structural change in church government or liturgical practice. But for many Puritan pastors

---

10 See 'Introduction' in John Coffey & Paul C H Lim (eds), *The Cambridge Companion to Puritanism* (Cambridge: Cambridge University Press, 2008).

the critical means to achieving true reform lay in faithful ministry in local contexts.[11] This was clearly the case for Baxter. While he did seek for structural reform in various ways, his key strategy was to focus on the conversion of individuals in the parish setting:

> I can well remember the time when I was earnest for the reformation of matters of ceremony ... Alas! Can we think that the reformation is wrought, when we cast out a few ceremonies, and changed some vestures, and gestures, and forms! Oh no, sirs! It is the converting and saving of souls that is our business. That is the chiefest part of reformation, that doth most good, and tendeth most to the salvation of the people.[12]

For Baxter, therefore, it was a case of reformation from below, not above. As he implemented this methodology in Kidderminster, and saw its effectiveness, he believed that the same approach could bear fruit throughout the nation. Baxter came to realise that there were certain key planks in achieving reform. And it was the pastor, as shepherd of the flock, who bore the core responsibility if such an outcome was to occur.

This is where *The Reformed Pastor* comes into play. This work was not simply an occasional writing. Rather, it set forth a blueprint for reforming England. It was the culmination of Baxter's reflection upon many years of ministry practice, outlining the principles and practicalities of the pastoral task.[13] The occasion that gave rise to the treatise itself was a sermon that Baxter had been asked to preach to a group of pastors. Fifty-eight ministers who shared Baxter's conviction of the necessity of pastoral involvement with the individual members of their congregations had written *The Agreement of divers Ministers of Christ in the County of Worcester ... for Catechizing* (1656). Aware of the enormity of such a task, these ministers agreed to hold a day of prayer and asked Baxter to preach. He was unable to attend due to illness, but

11 See Collinson, *Puritan Movement*, p 465; cf. Tom Webster, *Godly Clergy in Early Stuart England: The Caroline Puritan Movement, c. 1620-1643* (Cambridge: Cambridge University Press, 1997), pp 337-8.

12 Richard Baxter, *The Reformed Pastor* (Edinburgh: The Banner of Truth Trust, 1979 [abridged ed. 1829), p 211. This chapter will make use of the Banner of Truth edition of the abridged version of *The Reformed Pastor* since it is the most readily available version of the work.

13 J William Black, *Reformation Pastors: Richard Baxter and the Ideal of the Reformed Pastor* (Carlisle: Paternoster, 2004), pp 82-83.

he reworked his sermon and published it in an enlarged form.[14] The treatise is an extended exposition of Acts 20:28, the apostle Paul's exhortation to the elders in the Ephesian church to 'Keep watch over yourselves and over all the flock, of which the Holy Spirit has made you overseers.' We turn now to consider some of the central features of Baxter's understanding of the pastoral task as they emerge in this work.

5.3.2. *Key Directives for pastors*

Reform yourself

Baxter was convinced that if real change was to occur in the spiritual condition of England, it had to begin with the pastors. Those entrusted with this role bore a weighty responsibility. As preachers of the word of God they were God's agents for change, and they needed to be 'reformed' under that word before they could be human instruments to effect reformation in others. What, then, did they have to do? Essentially the task was to attend to their own spiritual lives:

> If it not be your daily business to study your own hearts, and to subdue corruption, and to walk with God – if you make not this a work to which you constantly attend, all will go wrong, and you will starve your hearers.[15]

There may have been elements of unhealthy introspection in Puritanism. But these concerns – to examine one's heart before God, to put sin to death, and to commune with God in prayer and meditation upon the Scriptures – were all essentials of ministerial life. Why was this the case? Because, Baxter claimed, 'that which is most on your hearts, is like to be most in their ears.'[16] In other words, the spiritual condition of the flock was intimately linked to that of their pastor.

In one section of *The Reformed Pastor*, Baxter outlines a number of sins to which pastors were especially prone.[17] There was the all too prevalent vice of pride. There was the danger of negligence in performing one's responsibilities, whether that be carelessness in study, a lack of liveliness in preaching, or in failing to take up opportunities to

---

[14] Paul C H Lim, 'The Reformed Pastor by Richard Baxter' in Kelly M Kapic & Randall C Gleason (eds), *The Devoted Life: An Invitation to the Puritan Classics* (Downers Grove, Ill.: IVP, 2004), pp 157-158.

[15] Baxter, *Reformed Pastor*, p 62.

[16] Baxter, *Reformed Pastor*, p 61.

[17] See Baxter, *Reformed Pastor*, pp 133-172. See also the discussion in Andrew Purves, *Pastoral Theology in the Classical Tradition* (Louisville, Kentucky: Westminster John Knox Press, 2001), pp 106-107.

assist congregations that were lacking ministerial oversight. Another temptation for pastors was worldly gain in whatever form that took, such as love of money or love of praise. Pastors could also adopt a divisive attitude that betrayed a lack of concern for the peace and unity of the church. Finally, Baxter believed that pastors were sadly negligent in exercising church discipline. All such sins needed attention with a spirit of repentance. 'It is time,' wrote Baxter, '... for us to take our part of that humiliation to which we have been so long calling our people.'[18] The critical point that Baxter is making, therefore, is that the word of God must do its work upon the shepherd if that word is to bear fruit amongst the flock. Godly character and obedient living were of the very essence of the ministerial task and could never be taken as mere optional extras.

Preach in a manner attuned to the nature of your hearers

Baxter had little time for preachers feted for their beautiful and sophisticated rhetoric, such as the Anglican, Lancelot Andrewes. His interest was in hearers who clearly grasped what the word of God was saying to them and would therefore know how to set themselves to the responsibilities of faithful Christian living. So, Baxter's preference was for what has come to be known as the Puritan plain style.[19] In response to a letter from a young minister, Baxter wrote:

> Study to preach to them as plainely seriously and movingly as you can speake. Let both your language & tone be as familiar as possible. Preach to them as you would discourse with them: & studiously avoid an affected, strained aliene tone ... In preaching and private dealing, be sure to manifest as much love to your hearers as you can; preach rather with tender melting affection, than with anger & disdaine. Speake to them loveingly as if they were your owne brethren.[20]

Baxter's point is that speaking in a natural, everyday manner assists the communication process. Preaching marked by eloquence or superior knowledge had more to do with showing off than with pastoral faithfulness. It was, quite simply, an act of selfishness.

The correspondence reveals another element that Baxter believed was necessary to effective preaching – emotional engagement. Passion

---

18 Baxter, *Reformed Pastor*, p 171.
19 Keeble, 'Baxter, Richard (1615-1691)', *ODNB*.
20 Keeble & Nuttall, *Calendar* Vol I, pp 146-7.

and a sense of urgency were required. Baxter was harsh in his criticism of dull preachers:

> A sleepy preacher will hardly awaken drowsy sinners. ... Speak to your people as to men that must be awakened ... the work is God's ... but yet his ordinary way is to work by means, and to make not only the matter that is preached, but also the manner of preaching instrumental to the work.[21]

While Baxter believed that any spiritual advancement was dependent upon divine acts of grace mediated through the Holy Spirit, he also held to the commonplace Puritan understanding that God usually conducted this work via the means of normal human functioning. God had designed human nature in such a way that action was driven by the affections of the heart. What one did was determined more by what one *loved* than by what one *understood.*[22] Hence the need for preaching that engaged hearers and challenged them to love the things that God loves and to hate what God hated. Preaching that simply presented facts, therefore, would never effectively elicit spiritual maturity.

Catechise the individuals under your care

Baxter's vision was large – he wanted to change a nation – but he was also ever alert to the one lost sheep. This truth is evident in his correspondence, whether it be offering counsel to a woman careworn with anxiety and depression or to a young man struggling with lustful thoughts. But his concern for the individual is best seen in his catechizing ministry. He recognised that in the context of teaching the faith to individuals and families he was able to work out whether or not people were converted and precisely what sort of instruction was necessary. For Baxter, the ministry of the word must not be limited to the pulpit.

Baxter settled upon a methodology that was time consuming. Catechisms would be delivered to families across the parish and they would be asked to study them. Then, four to six weeks later, each family would meet for one hour either with Baxter, or with his curate, Richard Sargeant, to be questioned and instructed in the essentials of the

---

21 Baxter, *Reformed Pastor*, pp 148-9.

22 For an extended discussion on Baxter's psychological understanding, see Keith Condie, 'Light Accompanied with Vital Heat': Affection and Intellect in the Thought of Richard Baxter' in Alec Ryrie & Tom Schwanda (eds), *Puritanism and Emotion in the Early Modern World* (London: Palgrave Macmillan, 2016), pp 13-46.

Christian faith.[23] The two men would spend Mondays and Tuesdays engaged in this work, catechizing approximately fourteen to sixteen families per week, or about 800 families per year.[24] The process enabled careful oversight of each individual's spiritual condition. Baxter wrote:

> I have found by experience, that some ignorant persons, who have been so long unprofitable hearers, have got more knowledge and remorse of conscience in half an hour's close discourse, than they did from ten years' public preaching.[25]

Baxter was thoroughly convinced, therefore, of the fruitfulness of this pastoral strategy. He did not view catechizing as an innovative practice. Rather, to his mind he was simply returning to the sort of ministerial work that characterised the early church.[26] It was another form of the ministry of the word and the knowledge gained of individuals in this context would inform the rest of his ministry and result in him being a better preacher.[27]

It appears that Baxter's catechizing ministry in Kidderminster did bear spiritual fruit. Years later he could reflect upon a work that had seen many converted and the village transformed:

> The congregation was usually full, so that we were fain to build five galleries after my coming thither. ... On the Lord's days ... you might hear an hundred families singing psalms and repeating sermons as you passed through the streets. ... When I came thither first there was about one family in a street that worshipped God ... and when I came away there were some streets where there was not past one Family in the side that did not so.[28]

Baxter's reflections upon his pastoral experience in Kidderminster and upon the apostle's charge in Acts 21 granted him a particular perspective upon how ministry ought to be conducted in local settings.

---

23 Baxter's assistant spent some weeks observing Baxter in the work of catechizing in order to train him for the task. Baxter described what he believed the key topics for discussion to be: 'The most that I insist on, of any one thinge, is a description of the new creature to them, & the nature & necessity of Sanctification; after the explication of the principall credenda.' See Keeble & Nuttall, *Calendar* I, p 238.

24 See Baxter, *Reformed Pastor,* pp 231-256; Baxter, *Reliquiae Baxterianae,* II. §41, pp 179-180; letter to John Eliot [approx.. January 1669] in Keeble & Nuttall, *Calendar* II, 69-70. See also the discussion in Kapic & Gleason, *The Devoted Life,* p 160.

25 Baxter, *Reformed Pastor,* p 196.

26 Baxter, *Reformed Pastor,* p 174.

27 Baxter, *Reformed Pastor,* p 177.

28 Baxter, *Reliquiae Baxterianae,* I. §136, pp 84-85.

He believed that the size of congregations should be limited so that the pastor could have personal knowledge of each parishioner.

> Flocks must ordinarily be no greater than we are capable of overseeing, or 'taking heed to'. ... If the pastoral office consists in overseeing all the flock, then surely the number of souls under the care of each pastor must not be greater than he is able to take such heed to as is here required.[29]

Such a perspective bears out the truth that, for Baxter, the spiritual state of every person under one's pastoral charge was a matter of great import. Catechizing, he believed, was a crucial means both to diagnose spiritual condition and to offer the instruction necessary to elicit further growth. It is no wonder that in later life he wrote, 'Of all the Works that I ever attempted, this yielded me the most Comfort in the practice of it.'[30]

Exercise church discipline

From the earliest days of his ministry, Baxter had expressed his concern that the Holy God was being dishonoured by a lack of effective church discipline. He opposed the '*promiscuous giving of the Lord's Supper to all Drunkards, Swearers, Fornicators, Scorners at Godliness* &c.'[31] And for Baxter, once again the corrective lay within the responsibilities of pastors:

> I confess, if I had my will, that man should be ejected as a negligent pastor, that will not rule his people by discipline, as well as he is ejected as a negligent preacher that will not preach; for ruling I am sure is as essential a part of the pastor's office as preaching.[32]

Full communicant members of the church were required to submit to discipline. Generally this meant that parishioners would be privately admonished for sins. But more severe cases would require public confession, with excommunication being the ultimate sanction.[33] A parish meeting was held on the first Wednesday of each month to oversee the disciplinary process.[34] In this way the holiness of life that Baxter was convinced was so necessary for the church of God would be

---

29 Baxter, *Reformed Pastor*, p 88. He expressed the same sentiment, with the qualification 'except publique Preachinge', in a letter to Thomas Wadsworth in 1656; see Keeble & Nuttall, *Calendar* I, p 202.

30 Baxter, *Reliquiae Baxterianae*, II. §41, p 179.

31 Baxter, *Reliquiae Baxterianae*, I. §19, p 14.

32 Baxter, *Reformed Pastor*, p 171.

33 See Baxter, *Reformed Pastor*, pp 104-111.

34 Baxter, *Reliquiae Baxterianae*, I. §135-137, pp 84-88.

maintained. But as mentioned above, for Baxter, church discipline was restorative, not merely punitive. Discipline that aimed merely to admonish and prevent participation at communion was nothing more than tyranny if not accompanied by the positive aspects of pastoral oversight such as instruction in the ways of godliness.[35]

Unite with other pastors

Baxter was deeply concerned about the break-up of Protestantism in England. He observed the emergence of a variety of sects and divisions amongst the nonconformists during the period of the Commonwealth and in subsequent years. Although a nonconformist himself, he longed for a national Church of England that would incorporate Protestants who were theologically orthodox but held disparate beliefs on non-essential matters. Baxter wrote numerous treatises arguing for church unity in the nation and some of his more theological writings were also related to this theme.[36] But Baxter's concern for unity was not simply theoretical; he also put it into practice. He gathered together other ministers in the local area and formed the Worcestershire Association. At their meetings each month they would share a meal, engage in a disputation upon a previously agreed topic, and, at times, would discuss matters of discipline.[37] As news spread of the benefits of this ministerial fellowship, other counties adopted this model and formed similar associations of pastors.[38] For Baxter, this was evidence of the very work of reformation that he longed for.[39]

---

35 Keeble, 'Baxter, Richard (1615-1691)' *ODNB*.

36 For example, his *Catholick Theologie* (London, 1675) was an attempt to promote peacefulness amongst those involved in doctrinal controversies and he argued that the differences between Calvinists and Arminians had more to do with the meaning of words than anything truly substantive. See also his comments in *Reformed Pastor*, pp 123-124.

37 Baxter, *Reliquiae Baxterianae*, I. §136, p 85. See also Keeble, 'Baxter, Richard (1615-1691)' *ODNB*.

38 John Spurr notes that clerical associations were formed in at least seventeen counties. See John Spurr, *English Puritanism 1603-1689* (Basingstoke: Macmillan, 1998), p 125. See also a letter from Baxter to John Eliot in Keeble & Nuttall, *Calendar* II, p 70 and William M Lamont, *Richard Baxter and the Millennium* (London: Croom Helm, 1979), p 165.

39 See letter from Baxter to John Eliot in Keeble & Nuttall, *Calendar* II, p 70; also N H Keeble, *'Loving & Free Converse': Richard Baxter in his Letters* (London: Dr. Williams's Trust, 1991), p 19.

5.3.3. *A case study of Baxter's application of the word of God: melancholia*[40]

I once spoke with a man who had struggled with mild depression in early adulthood. He had sought help from a variety of sources, including a number of books, but informed me that what he had found most helpful was the section on 'melancholia' in Baxter's *A Christian Directory*. Within this work he encountered biblical truth combined with wise advice that brought great personal benefit.

Whereas *The Reformed Pastor* articulates core principles of the pastoral task, *A Christian Directory* is Baxter's attempt to apply the theoretical knowledge gleaned from the Scriptures, along with 'natural truth', to all the situations of life.[41] In other words, it is 'a sum of practical theology', as he states in the subtitle to the work. Within Baxter's wide-ranging consideration of the sorts and conditions of human experience is a section entitled, 'Directions to the melancholy about their thoughts'. Baxter recognised that allowing our thinking or feelings to run free can have a significant impact upon us. Certain people can fall into depression 'by overstraining either their thoughts or their affections'.[42] He describes the condition with great accuracy – the fear and anxiety; the excessive sadness; the self-accusations; the feeling of being abandoned by God; the lack of joy; the accusing conscience; the social withdrawal – these and other signs and symptoms of clinical depression are clearly articulated by Baxter.[43]

The dominant emphasis within Baxter's practical writings is upon the duties of Christian living. But when he turns to provide advice to those burdened by the awful condition of melancholy, he lays more emphasis upon the consolations of grace than the responsibilities that flow from being recipients of that grace. So, for Baxter, it is important for sufferers to have a clear grasp of biblical truth. They need to ensure that 'no error in religion be the cause of your distress'. They need to understand that God is not only great, he also is totally good – that in his mercy 'he hath provided for all mankind so sufficient a Saviour' that anyone who 'penitently and believingly' responds to his gracious offer is completely pardoned of their sins. Baxter reduces the level of spiritual

40 'Melancholia' was the seventeenth-century term used to describe what today would be known as depression.

41 Richard Baxter, *A Christian Directory* (Morgan, PA: Soli Deo Gloria Publications, 1996 [1673]), p 557.

42 Baxter, *Christian Directory*, p 261.

43 Baxter, *Christian Directory*, pp 261-263.

demand: 'That the same thing which is a great duty to others, may be no duty to one, who by bodily distemper (as fevers, phrensies, melancholy) is unable to perform it.' Moreover, he cautions against spending lengthy time in meditating upon the Scriptures or in personal prayer, as such inward-focused activity can exacerbate their symptoms. In addition, those beset with melancholy ought not to worry too much about how they feel with regard to God and their spiritual state. Instead they should focus upon what they know to be true and seek to act upon this to the best of their ability, even if they don't feel like it. Baxter's wise counsel extends beyond Scriptural application. As a keen observer of human behaviour he was also attuned to other factors that influence the cause and progress of the state of melancholy – the place of temperament and personality; that patterns of thinking are not always trustworthy; the danger of being idle; the value of seeking medical assistance, etc.[44]

What is apparent from this brief case study, therefore, is that there is a level of sophistication in Baxter's pastoral work. His was a ministry that was theologically focused yet anthropologically aware. While the word of God is central to his approach, he also recognised that our embodiment has an impact upon all areas of human functioning and experience, including emotional and spiritual states. 'Are we not men before we are christians?' wrote Baxter.[45] This fact meant that knowledge that could be gained from observation and investigation should not be rejected. Within the framework of biblical authority, use could be made of such insights, for 'there are many natural truths which the Scripture meddleth not with.'[46] In fact, these natural truths bear the imprint of the divine hand that stands behind all of the created order. For Baxter, then, to pursue a faithful ministry of the word did not require the rejection of any truth that was not explicitly found in the Scriptures. Rather, such insights were to be appropriated alongside biblical teaching, when necessary, in order to provide the wisest counsel possible.

---

44 This paragraph is drawn from Baxter, *Christian Directory*, pp 264-267.

45 Baxter, *Christian Directory*, p 5.

46 Baxter, *Christian Directory*, p 557.

5.4. *Critical engagement with Baxter's approach to pastoral ministry*

5.4.1. *Theological error*

Earlier we noted Baxter's resistance to antinomianism, that is, to any teaching that downplayed the necessity of obedience to God's law. The living God was a holy God, and those called into his kingdom needed to heed his call to 'Be holy as I am holy' (Leviticus 19:2; 1 Peter 1:16). Baxter's strong reaction against antinomianism had a significant impact upon his understanding of the doctrine of justification. While convinced of the truth of the Protestant viewpoint, that salvation involved no human merit, he saw need for a doctrine of justification that provided an adequate ground for the believer to pursue holiness of life. The outcome was a system that placed great stress upon human responsibility in the life of faith, without that involvement being deemed meritorious in the sight of God.

In order to achieve this outcome, Baxter reformulated the covenant theology that was characteristic of Puritanism and other post-Reformation Protestant thought according to a 'political method'.[47] He believed that theology was concerned with the kingdom of God, and as such, needed to be understood in terms of the governmental and legal categories that characterise normal human society.[48] By utilising such a political framework, Baxter was able to formulate a view of God's law that was distinct from orthodox Calvinism. He believed that God's law was not grounded in his character (and thus immutable and eternal), but was merely the means by which he exercises his rule over his kingdom. This meant that God was free to change his law. In Baxter's governmental scheme, the work of Christ satisfied the law of the covenant of works, not as a substitute for fallen man, but in order to satisfy the lawgiver so that a new law might be put in its place. The requirements of this new law were within the ability of man to fulfil. Thus by obedience to this new and easier law, people could be restored to a proper relationship with their king.

What is the condition necessary to fulfil this new law, upon which justification could be granted? The condition is faith. But in order for

---

47 J I Packer, *The Redemption & Restoration of Man in the Thought of Richard Baxter* (Vancouver: Regent College Publishing, 2003 [1954]), p 213.

48 'Theology is the Doctrine of the Kingdom of God', in Baxter's 'To the Reader', in William Allen, *A Discourse of the Nature, Ends, and Difference of the Two Covenants* (London, 1673), sig. A2r.

one to continue in a state of justification, one must fulfil the duties implicit in the relationship to Christ which the first act of faith created: 'Faith, Repentance, Love, Thankfulness, sincere Obedience, together with finall Perseverance, do make up the Condition of our final Absolution in Judgement, and our eternal Glorification.'[49] For Baxter there is a two-fold righteousness necessary for salvation. The first is legal righteousness, attained through Christ's obedience that fulfils the law of works and enables the new covenant to be made. The second is the believer's evangelical righteousness, the fulfilment of the condition that qualifies the believer for salvation that the new covenant offers.[50]

For Baxter, this reformulation of the doctrine of justification was an essential means of undermining the Antinomian position. It provided a rationale for why the believer must live a holy life. For, if Christ's moral righteousness were imputed to believers (as is claimed in traditional Reformed thought), there would be no basis to require holiness, since Christ would have already fulfilled the law in their place. Baxter's position provided an unambiguous foundation for an obedient Christian lifestyle. It was, however, one of the main reasons why Baxter was constantly in the midst of controversy throughout his life, as this understanding of justification inflamed Protestant sensibilities as being too akin to the Roman Catholic position.

Every theological conviction carries a pastoral edge. Baxter's position on justification placed stress upon the duties required of one seeking to live faithfully for Christ. According to his schema, while the performance of these duties did not contribute to one's salvation, they were indicative of a true and lively faith. Baxter appears to have been fearful of expressing the notion of free grace in a manner that might encourage spiritual indolence or moral indulgence. What was the pastoral outcome from such a viewpoint? When the emphasis lies with the human will and what the believer must do, there is always the

---

49 Richard Baxter, *Rich. Baxter's Confession of his Faith* (London, 1655), p 56.

50 For full discussions of Baxter's doctrine of justification, see H Boersma, *A Hot Pepper Corn: Richard Baxter's Doctrine of Justification in its Seventeenth-Century Context of Controversy* (Zoetermeer: Uitgeverij Boekencentrum, 1993); Packer, *Redemption*, chapter 10; J V Fesko, *Beyond Calvin: Union with Christ and Justification in Early Modern Reformed Theology (1517-1700)* (Göttingen: Vandenhoeck & Ruprecht, 2012), chapter 16; J J Ballor, 'The Shape of Reformed Orthodoxy in the Seventeenth Century: The Soteriological Debate between George Kendall and Richard Baxter' in J J Ballor, D S Sytsma and J Zuidema (eds), *Church and School in Early Modern Protestantism: Studies in Honor of Richard A. Muller on the Maturation of a Theological Tradition* (Leiden: Brill, 2013), pp 665-678.

danger of moralism. In the words of Purves, Baxter's position 'has doubtful theological virtue, not least because it is in the end staggeringly unevangelical in its casting of persons back upon their own faith and obedience, rather than upon Christ.'[51] Therefore Baxter's attempt to promote holy living in the church resulted in the transposition of a central biblical doctrine in a manner that subtly undermined the achievement of the protestant reformation.

5.4.2. *Rhetorical impact*

Even if Baxter's soteriological system was essentially grace based as he claimed, it appears that grace was not the dominant message received by many who read his books. The stress upon the duties requisite upon the believer led some to feel spiritually overwhelmed by what was being asked of them.[52] Baxter did write of divine grace and empowerment, and of the weakness of the human soul in serving God, ideas that could potentially ease the sense of burden upon troubled consciences. But it appears that these motifs were drowned out by a more dominant theme: that good deeds and holy living were the great marks of those who were truly redeemed, and that earnest application to devotional practices and duties (such as bible reading, prayer, meeting with other believers, self-examination, meditation, etc.), were the marks of authentic holiness. Furthermore, it was often difficult for individuals to distinguish whether or not they were fulfilling these duties to an adequate standard. Believers were encouraged to engage in self-examination to see whether or not they were displaying the appropriate fruit of a regenerate life, but it was often easier to detect inadequacies than to see small steps of progress. This could lead to an oppressive sense of failure, especially for those of tender conscience. In sum, it appears that the consolatory message of God's grace to human sinners was not always the dominant message communicated to those who fell under Baxter's pastoral sway.

This outcome was not unique to Baxter, and it has been suggested that this was a key weakness of Puritan piety. Scholars such as Stachniewski, Como & Bozeman have argued that embedded within the design of Puritan practical divinity with its intense focus upon sanctification lay some harmful spiritual and psychological

---

51 Purves, *Pastoral Theology*, p 110.

52 For examples and discussion that bears upon the contents of this section, see Keith Condie, 'The Theory, Practice, and Reception of Meditation in the Thought of Richard Baxter' (PhD Thesis, University of Sydney, 2010), chapter 5.

consequences.[53] David Como describes the impact of the tension between the life of grace and the demands of holy living upon some Puritans in these terms:

> Although ... [the] mainstream mode of piety seemed to have proved sufficient for the large majority of godly people, there can be little question that for some men and women, the disciplines, demands, and general tenor of normative Puritanism proved to be a passageway into despair and insecurity.[54]

To be fair, for Baxter, the impact of this tendency was somewhat attenuated when dealing with people on a one-to-one basis. When catechizing or corresponding he had the ability to modify the hard edge that is apparent in much of his published work and to offer pastoral advice that took account of individual differences.[55] But this discussion alerts us to the fact that careful pastoral work recognises that words can carry unintended meanings and therefore pays attention, not only to what is said, but to how it is said.

There is also some evidence that Baxter's rhetoric laid too heavy a burden, not only upon lay folk, but also upon those engaged in the pastoral task. Thomas Gouldstone was the Rector of the parish of Finchley in Middlesex. A year or two after the publication of *The Reformed Pastor* he wrote to Baxter:

> Sir I thanke you for your *Gildas Salvianus*<: *The Reformed Pastor* (1656)> & with my soule wish I were able to putt it in practice: that my wish is hearty I hope I shall show it by endeavouring my uttermost but the truth is that was calculated aright for the meridian of Kederminster not of ffinchly. I buckle under the burthen.[56]

Here was a man convinced of the value of Baxter's methodology at the level of theory, but clearly was struggling to apply it in practice. Perhaps it could be argued that the problem was with the method itself rather than with how that method was communicated. But it appears that the way that Baxter expressed himself in his treatise did not grant this

---

[53] John Stachniewski, *The Persecutory Imagination: English Puritanism and the Literature of Religious Despair* (Oxford: Clarendon Press, 1991); David Como, *Blown by the Spirit: Puritanism and the Emergence of an Antinomian Underground in Pre-Civil-War England* (Stanford: Stanford University Press, 2004); Theodore D Bozeman, *The Precisianist Strain: Disciplinary Religion & Antinomian Backlash in Puritanism to 1638* (Chapel Hill: University of North Carolina Press, 2004).

[54] Como, *Blown by the Spirit*, p 37.

[55] See further, Condie, 'Meditation', chapter 5.

[56] Keeble & Nuttall, *Calendar* I, p 297.

minister a sufficient 'out' if different contextual variables rendered the method impossible to fulfil.

5.4.3. *Self-awareness*

As one gets to know Baxter through reading his autobiography, his treatises and correspondence, and the writings of contemporaries who knew him, perhaps it could be claimed that self-awareness was not his forte. Much of what he said and did appears to have been driven by his personality and experience, and at least some of the time he appeared to be blind to this. Baxter seems to have been easily affronted by criticism from others, yet was quite prepared to offer sharp rebuke to any he thought might be at fault.[57] For a man who was deeply committed to the unity of the church and thought that many controversies were unnecessary, he certainly played his part in creating them! Moreover, he believed that he was right in his opinions about most things and was confident in his ability to find the defects in the theological systems of others.[58] In addition, he was a man who locked in on details, not realising how this could hamstring the achievement of greater goals. For example, during the Savoy Conference of 1661 that was convened after the Restoration to review the *Book of Common Prayer*, Baxter debated every disputed point in such a way that irritated many of the delegates. Robert Sanderson, Bishop of Lincoln, is reported to have said of Baxter, 'he had never met with a man of more pertinacious confidence, and less abilities in all his conversation'.[59] In his writings he tended to verbosity, failing to follow his own advice that 'Overdoing is the ordinary way of Undoing.'[60]

Baxter, however, was not entirely unteachable and he learned from experience as he progressed in years. He realised that as a younger man he had been too on edge at his lack of a university education, and was thankful that God in his providence had 'bred me up in a more humbling way.'[61] He also came to appreciate that he had expressed some of his ideas too strongly: 'I have perceived, that nothing so much

---

57 Cf. Keeble, *Loving & Free Converse*, pp 10-15.

58 Baxter, *Reliquiae Baxterianae*, III, 69: 'I never yet saw a Scheme, or Method of Physicks or Theology, which gave satisfaction to my Reason ... I could never see any whose Confusion, or great Defects, I could not easily discover, but not so easily amend.'

59 Izaak Walton, *The lives of John Donne, Sir Henry Wotton, Richard Hooker, George Herbert, and Robert Sanderson*, (Oxford: Oxford University Press, new edition 1927, reprinted 1956), p 404, quoted in Keeble, *ODNB*.

60 Baxter, *Reliquiae Baxterianae*, I, § 40, p 27.

61 Richard Baxter, *Richard Baxter's Penitent Confession* (London, 1691), p 9.

hindreth the Reception of the Truth, as urging it on Men with too harsh Importunity, and falling too heavily on their Errors'.[62] In addition, Baxter acknowledged that there were some dangers in the Puritan emphasis upon looking inward. This had been his own focus during his younger years. But his later claim was that the time spent in examination of his own sins and spiritual state would have been better spent with an outward gospel focus: 'I see more need of a higher work; and that I should look often upon Christ, and God, and Heaven, than upon my own Heart.'[63] Overall, however, it would be fair to say that a little more emotional intelligence on Baxter's part might have issued in an even more fruitful ministry.

5.5. *Appropriating Baxter today?*

5.5.1. *The 'always reforming' pastor*

Ministry today is no easy task. It requires a complex set of skills in a demanding world. What does a pastor need to fulfil this role with faithfulness? A couple of initial comments might help set the scene. First, Andrew Purves notes that much current pastoral theology literature is more focused upon a pastor's mental health than upon his spiritual renewal.[64] Such an emphasis is not entirely out of place. Burnout is a real phenomenon and some wisdom in handling stress is important. But should this area of concern be the dominating motif in theological reflection upon the pastoral task? Second, I once spoke with a minister about his experience of interviewing applicants to assist him in the pastoral work of the church. He would explain the nature of the role, and then ask if the interviewee had any questions. Most of the time the first question asked was, 'What's the pay?' Again, this is not an unreasonable question, but perhaps it reveals something of the priorities of the enquirer.

An earlier section of this chapter outlined Baxter's answer to our question. For him, faithful Christian ministry issues from pastors whose dominant focus is their own spiritual condition – whose 'daily business' is, as he urged his readers, 'to study your own hearts, and to subdue corruption, and to walk with God'.[65] The word 'mortification' is

---

[62] Baxter, *Reliquiae Baxterianae*, I, § 213, p 125.
[63] Baxter, *Reliquiae Baxterianae*, I, § 213, p 129.
[64] Purves, *Pastoral Theology*, pp 105-106.
[65] Baxter, *Reformed Pastor*, p 62.

almost lost to modern evangelicalism. Is the concept also in decline? Are we interested in fighting sin? Do we know how to do so? Will God bless ministry under a pastor who is greedy, who is not gentle, or who is addicted to pornography? Do we believe that Christian character is the one non-negotiable requirement for those in pastoral ministry? Is godliness of life the characteristic that pastors are most known for? For Baxter, the answers to such questions really matter. A shepherd over God's flock will bring no true benefit to others unless his own spiritual life is in order.

5.5.2. *The evangelistic imperative*

Baxter loved the lost and prayed for the lost. He wrote treatises that were extended tracts, written with the aim of convincing unbelievers to come to Christ. While we have spoken of his desire to see England transformed by the word of God, his vision was cast large and he had a missionary heart. In his autobiography he wrote:

> I cannot be affected so much with the Calamities of my own Relations, or the Land of my Nativity, as with the Case of the Heathen, Mahometan, and ignorant Nations of the Earth. No part of my Prayers are so deeply serious, as that for the Conversion of the Infidel and Ungodly World'.[66]

This concern for worldwide evangelism led Baxter to take a particular interest in the work of John Eliot. Eliot had emigrated to New England and exercised a significant ministry to the Indians of Massachusetts, including translating the Bible into their language. In correspondence with Eliot, Baxter states, 'I know no worke in all the world that I thinke more highly & honourably of than yours; & consequently no person whom I more honour for his worke sake.'[67] Baxter's heartfelt desires for those far and wide without knowledge of Christ are an encouragement for us to recapture an urgent concern for the lost.

5.5.3. *Understanding people*

The Puritans, Baxter included, had a sophisticated understanding of human functioning and made use of their insights in their ministry of the word of God. It was not adequate simply to engage the human intellect and will. In other words, more was needed than providing information to people and then telling them what to do. Central to

---

66 Baxter, *Reliquiae Baxterianae*, I, § 213, p 131.

67 Keeble & Nuttall, *Calendar* I, p 240.

Puritan thought was the notion that human beings are creatures who must worship. In the fallen condition, rather than worshiping the true and living God, we lapse into idolatry and turn to false gods – material things, pleasure, reputation, etc. – to provide meaning and satisfaction in life. How do these idols wield their power over us? By means of our desires, imaginations and feelings. A sinful desire gains a foothold through the imagination, which paints pictures in our minds of how attractive it would be to fulfil that desire. These imaginations then stir our emotions and move our wills, and before we know it, we have succumbed to sinful action. For the Puritans, therefore, what was needed was to preach the word of God in a manner that desires, imaginations and affections were locked on to God. Hearts needed to be captured so that God was loved above all else. Desires and affections needed to be re-ordered so that we love what God loves and hate what he hates. And central to this task was the role of the imagination, that faculty of the human soul that could provide a vision of the majesty and goodness of God and of the horror of sin. When the mind's eye was filled with such conceptions, desires would be altered and affections would be moved to produce the fruit of a godly life.[68] Baxter's employment of these principles of how we function as human beings is evident throughout his treatises and correspondence. He was able to apply his understanding of human nature to a vast array of life situations. Moreover, he did so with wisdom and grace. As one writer has noted, '[a]lmost always there is the combination of sanity with deep concern.'[69] Baxter provides a helpful reminder that faithful ministry of the word of God is never merely the sharing of information and that true knowledge of God is much more than knowledge about him.

5.5.4. *Every sheep matters*

The central principle that undergirded Baxter's model of pastoral catechesis was a concern for the spiritual state of every individual: the need to take care of all the flock. The model was developed in a particular context – village life in seventeenth-century England. To think that his approach could be easily replicated in the variety of twenty-first

68 For further discussion of the role of the affections and imagination in Puritan thought, see Timothy J Keller, 'Puritan Resources for Biblical Counseling', *Journal of Pastoral Practice* 9 (1988), pp 11-44; Keith Condie, 'The Puritans, Theological Anthropology and Emotions' in Michael P. Jensen (ed.), *True Feelings: Perspectives on emotions in Christian life and ministry* (Nottingham: Apollos, 2012).

69 Geoffrey F Nuttall, *The Puritan Spirit: Essays and Addresses* (London: Epworth Press, 1967), p 112.

century ministry settings would be a mistake. Yet adaptations have been made to good effect. For example, Wallace Benn reworked the model for use with a youth fellowship group and also with members of a church in suburban London.[70] One-to-one ministry is used by many to good effect today. Often the participants read the bible together in discipleship or mentoring contexts. But might not such meetings also be used for diagnostic purposes, to assess spiritual health and determine possible ways to move forward? One-to-one ministry is an activity that any Christian person can engage in and ought not to be limited to pastoral staff. Those in leadership positions cannot do everything. What Baxter reminds us of, however, is that shepherds of God's flock need to be concerned for every sheep under their care. It is possible for pastors to distance themselves from their people. They can be so focused on the strategic target that effective ministry to the 'little person' is overlooked. Baxter would warn against such an approach to ministerial practice.

5.5.5. *Theology feeds and shapes pastoral ministry*

Baxter's pastoral work was grounded upon fundamental theological truths. It was driven by soteriological and eschatological concerns – the need for people to be saved and to be guided safely to heaven. And undergirding these concerns was a Christological priority, the fact that it is the work of Christ that is central in the achievement of God's gracious redemptive purposes.[71] Any pastoral work that seeks to be biblical requires this focus.

But Baxter's ministry also demonstrates the pastoral outcomes that issue from theology which deviates from God's revelation in Scripture. He reacted to the Antinomian error with another error, and both of these mistakes had pastoral consequences. Antinomianism could so easily slip into licentiousness and thereby damage the purity of Christ's church. Yet Baxter's neo-nomianism carried the seeds of legalism with the potential to undermine assurance.

In his book, *Antinomianism,* Mark Jones notes that both Antinomians and Reformed theologians agreed that good works made no contribution to our justification. But he asks the question, is the gospel synonymous with the doctrine of justification or does it entail more than just this one doctrine? Puritans such as Samuel Rutherford,

---

70 Wallace Benn, *The Baxter Model: Guidelines for pastoring today* (Histon, Cambridge: Fellowship of Word and Spirit, 1993).

71 See Purves, *Pastoral Theology*, p 110.

John Owen and Thomas Manton typically referred to the gospel in a broader sense that also included the application of the gospel in the life of the believer. The gospel actually commands believers in matters of holiness. Perfection is not required, but a changed heart will result in a changed life. In other words, the pursuit of holiness is not simply an optional extra that can be elided from the soteriology found in the New Testament. Thus there is a sense in which it can be argued that good works *are* necessary for salvation.[72] Similarly, Jones demonstrates that there was a lack of theological sophistication in the manner in which Antinomians spoke of the love of God. It is simplistic to claim that, for those in Christ, God sees no sin in us and therefore he cannot love us more or less than he already does. Rather, we ought to take note of the careful distinctions employed by Reformed theologians that recognise that there are different forms of God's love. While God's benevolent love is unchanging, his complacent love, that is, God's pleasure or love of friendship or delight, can change depending upon the behaviour of the Christian. This second category explains Scriptural passages that speak of the believer pleasing God.[73] In thinking through the theological excesses of the seventeenth-century and applying them to today, Jones believes that we can be prone to the same reactionary tendencies that caused fault in Baxter: 'In our zeal against errors and heresies, we are perhaps the ones most vulnerable to infelicitous statements and hyperbolic rhetoric that often creates more heat than light.'[74]

All in all, Baxter challenges us to affirm the value of theology – good, healthy, biblically sourced theology. We are challenged to see the importance of good theological education, especially for those in pastoral ministry. And there is also the encouragement for pastors to be life-long learners so that they remain well-resourced to feed the flock and guard it from error.

5.6. *Conclusion*

Richard Baxter's approach to the pastoral task was strategic rather than naïve. He carefully observed the context of his church and country,

72 This material is drawn from Mark Jones, *Antinomianism: Reformed Theology's Unwelcome Guest?* (Phillipsburg, NJ: P&R Publishing, 2013), chapters 4-5. See also Bradley G Green, *Covenant and Commandment: Works, obedience and faithfulness in the Christian life* (NSBT 33; Nottingham: Apollos, 2014).

73 See Jones, *Antinomianism*, chap 6.

74 Jones, *Antinomianism*, pp 12-13.

came up with a plan for effective ministry in this context, and then worked hard at that plan. Although turbulent political and ecclesiological circumstances impeded his larger vision for the nation, and brought an end to his direct pastoral oversight in Kidderminster, his achievement ought not to be underestimated. His was a ministry centred on the word of God. He was a pastor committed to allowing that word to shape his own life as well as keeping that word as the content of his preaching and teaching. The conversion of sinners was a prime concern. But his system of catechesis enabled him not only to lead many to Christ, but also to see them built up in the faith. His model of pastoral ministry as expounded in *The Reformed Pastor* continues to challenge and inspire today. Like Baxter's contemporary, William Wadsworth, whose commendation we noted at the start of the chapter, we await the day when many will rise up and bless God for his work.

5.7. *Bibliography*

J J Ballor, 'The Shape of Reformed Orthodoxy in the Seventeenth Century: The Soteriological Debate between George Kendall and Richard Baxter' in J J Ballor, D S Sytsma and J Zuidema (eds), *Church and School in Early Modern Protestantism: Studies in Honor of Richard A. Muller on the Maturation of a Theological Tradition* (Leiden: Brill, 2013)

R Baxter, *Rich. Baxter's Confession of his Faith* (London, 1655)

———, *Catholick Theologie* (London, 1675)

———, 'To the Reader', in William Allen, *A Discourse of the Nature, Ends, and Difference of the Two Covenants* (London, 1673)

———, *Poetical Fragments* (London, 1681)

———, *Richard Baxter's Penitent Confession* (London, 1691)

———, *Reliquiae Baxterianae* (London, 1696)

———, *The Reformed Pastor* (Edinburgh: The Banner of Truth Trust, 1979 [abridged ed. 1829)

———, *A Christian Directory* (Morgan, PA: Soli Deo Gloria Publications, 1996 [1673])

W Benn, *The Baxter Model: Guidelines for pastoring today* (Histon, Cambridge: Fellowship of Word and Spirit, 1993)

J W Black, *Reformation Pastors: Richard Baxter and the Ideal of the Reformed Pastor* (Carlisle: Paternoster, 2004)

H Boersma, *A Hot Pepper Corn: Richard Baxter's Doctrine of Justification in its Seventeenth-Century Context of Controversy* (Zoetermeer: Uitgeverij Boekencentrum, 1993)

T D Bozeman, *The Precisianist Strain: Disciplinary Religion & Antinomian Backlash in Puritanism to 1638* (Chapel Hill: University of North Carolina Press, 2004)

J Coffey & P C H Lim (eds), *The Cambridge Companion to Puritanism* (Cambridge: Cambridge University Press, 2008)

P Collinson, *The Elizabethan Puritan Movement* (London: Jonathan Cape, 1967)

D Como, *Blown by the Spirit: Puritanism and the Emergence of an Antinomian Underground in Pre-Civil-War England* (Stanford: Stanford University Press, 2004)

K Condie, 'The Theory, Practice, and Reception of Meditation in the Thought of Richard Baxter' (PhD Thesis, University of Sydney, 2010)

———, 'The Puritans, Theological Anthropology and Emotions' in Michael P. Jensen (ed.), *True Feelings: Perspectives on emotions in Christian life and ministry* (Nottingham: Apollos, 2012)

———, 'Light Accompanied with Vital Heat': Affection and Intellect in the Thought of Richard Baxter' in Alec Ryrie & Tom Schwanda (eds), *Puritanism and Emotion in the Early Modern World* (London: Palgrave Macmillan, 2016)

T Cooper, 'Richard Baxter and his Physicians', *Social History of Medicine* 20 (2007), pp 1-19

———, *John Owen, Richard Baxter and the Formation of Nonconformity* (Farnham, Surrey: Ashgate, 2011)

J V Fesko, *Beyond Calvin: Union with Christ and Justification in Early Modern Reformed Theology (1517-1700)* (Göttingen: Vandenhoeck & Ruprecht, 2012)

B G Green, *Covenant and Commandment: Works, obedience and faithfulness in the Christian life* (NSBT 33; Nottingham: Apollos, 2014)

M Jones, *Antinomianism: Reformed Theology's Unwelcome Guest?* (Phillipsburg, NJ: P&R Publishing, 2013)

N H Keeble, *'Loving & Free Converse': Richard Baxter in his Letters* (London: Dr. Williams's Trust, 1991)

———, 'Baxter, Richard (1615-1691)', *Oxford Dictionary of National Biography*, (Oxford University Press, 2004); online edn, Jan 2008

——— & G F Nuttall, *Calendar of the Correspondence of Richard Baxter* (2 vols; Oxford: Oxford University Press, 1991)

Timothy J Keller, 'Puritan Resources for Biblical Counseling', *Journal of Pastoral Practice* 9 (1988), pp 11-44

W M Lamont, *Richard Baxter and the Millennium* (London: Croom Helm, 1979)

P C H Lim, '*The Reformed Pastor* by Richard Baxter' in Kelly M Kapic & Randall C Gleason (eds), *The Devoted Life: An Invitation to the Puritan Classics* (Downers Grove, Ill.: IVP, 2004)

G F Nuttall, *The Puritan Spirit: Essays and Addresses* (London: Epworth Press, 1967)

J I Packer, *The Redemption & Restoration of Man in the Thought of Richard Baxter* (Vancouver: Regent College Publishing, 2003 [1954])

A Purves, *Pastoral Theology in the Classical Tradition* (Louisville, Kentucky: Westminster John Knox Press, 2001)

J Spurr, *English Puritanism 1603-1689* (Basingstoke: Macmillan, 1998)

J Stachniewski, *The Persecutory Imagination: English Puritanism and the Literature of Religious Despair* (Oxford: Clarendon Press, 1991)

I Walton, *The lives of John Donne, Sir Henry Wotton, Richard Hooker, George Herbert, and Robert Sanderson*, (Oxford: Oxford University Press, new edition 1927, reprinted 1956)

T Webster, *Godly Clergy in Early Stuart England: The Caroline Puritan Movement, c. 1620-1643* (Cambridge: Cambridge University Press, 1997)

Index

Latimer Studies

LS 01	*The Evangelical Anglican Identity Problem*	Jim Packer
LS 02	*The ASB Rite A Communion: A Way Forward*	Roger Beckwith
LS 03	*The Doctrine of Justification in the Church of England*	Robin Leaver
LS 04	*Justification Today: The Roman Catholic and Anglican Debate*	R. G. England
LS 05/06	*Homosexuals in the Christian Fellowship*	David Atkinson
LS 07	*Nationhood: A Christian Perspective*	O. R. Johnston
LS 08	*Evangelical Anglican Identity: Problems and Prospects*	Tom Wright
LS 09	*Confessing the Faith in the Church of England Today*	Roger Beckwith
LS 10	*A Kind of Noah's Ark? The Anglican Commitment to Comprehensiveness*	Jim Packer
LS 11	*Sickness and Healing in the Church*	Donald Allister
LS 12	*Rome and Reformation Today: How Luther Speaks to the New Situation*	James Atkinson
LS 13	*Music as Preaching: Bach, Passions and Music in Worship*	Robin Leaver
LS 14	*Jesus Through Other Eyes: Christology in a Multi-faith Context*	Christopher Lamb
LS 15	*Church and State Under God*	James Atkinson,
LS 16	*Language and Liturgy*	Gerald Bray, Steve Wilcockson, Robin Leaver
LS 17	*Christianity and Judaism: New Understanding, New Relationship*	James Atkinson
LS 18	*Sacraments and Ministry in Ecumenical Perspective*	Gerald Bray
LS 19	*The Functions of a National Church*	Max Warren
LS19_2	*British Values and the National Church: Essays on Church and State from 1964-2014*	ed. David Holloway
LS 20/21	*The Thirty-Nine Articles: Their Place and Use Today*	Jim Packer, Roger Beckwith
LS 22	*How We Got Our Prayer Book*	T.W. Drury, Roger Beckwith
LS 23/24	*Creation or Evolution: a False Antithesis?*	Mike Poole, Gordon Wenham
LS 25	*Christianity and the Craft*	Gerard Moate
LS 26	*ARCIC II and Justification*	Alister McGrath
LS 27	*The Challenge of the Housechurches*	Tony Higton, Gilbert Kirby
LS 28	*Communion for Children? The Current Debate*	A. A. Langdon
LS 29/30	*Theological Politics*	Nigel Biggar
LS 31	*Eucharistic Consecration in the First Four Centuries and its Implications for Liturgical Reform*	Nigel Scotland
LS 32	*A Christian Theological Language*	Gerald Bray
LS 33	*Mission in Unity: The Bible and Missionary Structures*	Duncan McMann
LS 34	*Stewards of Creation: Environmentalism in the Light of Biblical Teaching*	Lawrence Osborn
LS 35/36	*Mission and Evangelism in Recent Thinking: 1974-1986*	Robert Bashford
LS 37	*Future Patterns of Episcopacy: Reflections in Retirement*	Stuart Blanch
LS 38	*Christian Character: Jeremy Taylor and Christian Ethics Today*	David Scott
LS 39	*Islam: Towards a Christian Assessment*	Hugh Goddard
LS 40	*Liberal Catholicism: Charles Gore and the Question of Authority*	G. F. Grimes
LS 41/42	*The Christian Message in a Multi-faith Society*	Colin Chapman
LS 43	*The Way of Holiness 1: Principles*	D. A. Ousley
LS 44/45	*The Lambeth Articles*	V. C. Miller

LS 46	*The Way of Holiness 2: Issues*	D. A. Ousley
LS 47	*Building Multi-Racial Churches*	John Root
LS 48	*Episcopal Oversight: A Case for Reform*	David Holloway
LS 49	*Euthanasia: A Christian Evaluation*	Henk Jochemsen
LS 50/51	*The Rough Places Plain: AEA 1995*	
LS 52	*A Critique of Spirituality*	John Pearce
LS 53/54	*The Toronto Blessing*	Martyn Percy
LS 55	*The Theology of Rowan Williams*	Garry Williams
LS 56/57	*Reforming Forwards? The Process of Reception and the Consecration of Woman as Bishops*	Peter Toon
LS 58	*The Oath of Canonical Obedience*	Gerald Bray
LS 59	*The Parish System: The Same Yesterday, Today And For Ever?*	Mark Burkill
LS 60	*'I Absolve You': Private Confession and the Church of England*	Andrew Atherstone
LS 61	*The Water and the Wine: A Contribution to the Debate on Children and Holy Communion*	Roger Beckwith, Andrew Daunton-Fear
LS 62	*Must God Punish Sin?*	Ben Cooper
LS 63	*Too Big For Words? The Transcendence of God and Finite Human Speech*	Mark D. Thompson
LS 64	*A Step Too Far: An Evangelical Critique of Christian Mysticism*	Marian Raikes
LS 65	*The New Testament and Slavery: Approaches and Implications*	Mark Meynell
LS 66	*The Tragedy of 1662: The Ejection and Persecution of the Puritans*	Lee Gatiss
LS 67	*Heresy, Schism & Apostasy*	Gerald Bray
LS 68	*Paul in 3D: Preaching Paul as Pastor, Story-teller and Sage*	Ben Cooper
LS69	*Christianity and the Tolerance of Liberalism: J.Gresham Machen and the Presbyterian Controversy of 1922-1937*	Lee Gatiss
LS70	*An Anglican Evangelical Identity Crisis: The Churchman–Anvil Affair of 1981-4*	Andrew Atherstone
LS71	*Empty and Evil: The worship of other faiths in 1 Corinthians 8-10 and today*	Rohintan Mody
LS72	*To Plough or to Preach: Mission Strategies in New Zealand during the 1820s*	Malcolm Falloon
LS73	*Plastic People: How Queer Theory is changing us*	Peter Sanlon
LS74	*Deification and Union with Christ: Salvation in Orthodox and Reformed thought*	Slavko Eždenci
LS75	*As It Is Written: Interpreting the Bible with Boldness*	Benjamin Sargent
LS76	*Light From Dark Ages? An Evangelical Critique of Celtic Spirituality*	Marian Raikes
LS77	*The Ethics of Usury*	Ben Cooper
LS78	*For Us and For Our Salvation: 'Limited Atonement' in the Bible, Doctrine, History and Ministry*	Lee Gatiss
LS79	*Positive Complementarianism: The Key Biblical Texts*	Ben Cooper
LS80	*Were they preaching 'Another Gospel'? Justification by Faith I the Second Century*	Andrew Daunton-Fear
LS81	*Thinking Aloud: Responding to the Contemporary Debate about Marriage, Sexuality and Reconciliation*	Martin Davie
LS82	*Spells, Sorcerers and Spirits: Magic and the Occult in the Bible*	Kirsten Birkett
LS83	*Your Will Be Done: Exploring Eternal Subordination, Divine Monarchy and Divine Humility*	Michael J Ovey
LS84	*Resilience: A Spiritual Project*	Kirsten Birkett

	Latimer Briefings	
LB01	*The Church of England: What it is, and what it stands for*	R. T. Beckwith
LB02	*Praying with Understanding: Explanations of Words and Passages in the Book of Common Prayer*	R. T. Beckwith
LB03	*The Failure of the Church of England? The Church, the Nation and the Anglican Communion*	A. Pollard
LB04	*Towards a Heritage Renewed*	H.R.M. Craig
LB05	*Christ's Gospel to the Nations: The Heart & Mind of Evangelicalism Past, Present & Future*	Peter Jensen
LB06	*Passion for the Gospel: Hugh Latimer (1485–1555) Then and Now. A commemorative lecture to mark the 450th anniversary of his martyrdom in Oxford*	A. McGrath
LB07	*Truth and Unity in Christian Fellowship*	Michael Nazir-Ali
LB08	*Unworthy Ministers: Donatism and Discipline Today*	Mark Burkill
LB09	*Witnessing to Western Muslims: A Worldview Approach to Sharing Faith*	Richard Shumack
LB10	*Scarf or Stole at Ordination? A Plea for the Evangelical Conscience*	Andrew Atherstone
LB11	*How to Write a Theology Essay*	Michael P. Jensen
LB12	*Preaching: A Guidebook for Beginners*	Allan Chapple
LB13	*Justification by Faith: Orientating the Church's teaching and practice to Christ (Toon Lecture 1)*	Michael Nazir-Ali
LB14	*"Remember Your Leaders": Principles and Priorities for Leaders from Hebrews 13*	Wallace Benn
LB15	*How the Anglican Communion came to be and where it is going*	Michael Nazir-Ali
LB16	*Divine Allurement: Cranmer's Comfortable Words*	Ashley Null
LB17	*True Devotion: In Search of Authentic Spirituality*	Allan Chapple
LB18	*Commemorating War & Praying for Peace: A Christian Reflection on the Armed Forces*	John Neal

	Anglican Foundations Series	
FWC	*The Faith We Confess: An Exposition of the 39 Articles*	Gerald Bray
AF02	*The 'Very Pure Word of God': The Book of Common Prayer as a Model of Biblical Liturgy*	Peter Adam
AF03	*Dearly Beloved: Building God's People Through Morning and Evening Prayer*	Mark Burkill
AF04	*Day by Day: The Rhythm of the Bible in the Book of Common Prayer*	Benjamin Sargent
AF05	*The Supper: Cranmer and Communion*	Nigel Scotland
AF06	*A Fruitful Exhortation: A Guide to the Homilies*	Gerald Bray
AF07	*Instruction in the Way of the Lord: A Guide to the Prayer Book Catechism*	Martin Davie
AF08	*Till Death Us Do Part: "The Solemnization of Matrimony" in the Book of Common Prayer*	Simon Vibert
AF09	*Sure and Certain Hope: Death and Burial in the Book of Common Prayer*	Andrew Cinnamond

	Latimer Books	
GGC	*God, Gays and the Church: Human Sexuality and Experience in Christian Thinking*	eds. Lisa Nolland, Chris Sugden, Sarah Finch
WTL	*The Way, the Truth and the Life: Theological Resources for a Pilgrimage to a Global Anglican Future*	eds. Vinay Samuel, Chris Sugden, Sarah Finch
AEID	*Anglican Evangelical Identity – Yesterday and Today*	J.I.Packer, N.T.Wright
IB	*The Anglican Evangelical Doctrine of Infant Baptism*	John Stott, Alec Motyer
BF	*Being Faithful: The Shape of Historic Anglicanism Today*	Theological Resource Group of GAFCON
TPG	*The True Profession of the Gospel: Augustus Toplady and Reclaiming our Reformed Foundations*	Lee Gatiss
SG	*Shadow Gospel: Rowan Williams and the Anglican Communion Crisis*	Charles Raven
TTB	*Translating the Bible: From William Tyndale to King James*	Gerald Bray
PWS	*Pilgrims, Warriors, and Servants: Puritan Wisdom for Today's Church*	ed. Lee Gatiss
PPA	*Preachers, Pastors, and Ambassadors: Puritan Wisdom for Today's Church*	ed. Lee Gatiss
CWP	*The Church, Women Bishops and Provision: The Integrity of Orthodox Objections to the Proposed Legislation Allowing Women Bishops*	
TSF	*The Truth Shall Set You Free: Global Anglicans in the 21st Century*	ed. Charles Raven
LMM	*Launching Marsden's Mission: The Beginnings of the Church Missionary Society in New Zealand, viewed from New South Wales*	eds. Peter G Bolt David B. Pettett
MST1	*Listen To Him: Reading and Preaching Emmanuel in Matthew*	ed. Peter Bolt
GWC	*The Genius of George Whitefield: Reflections on his Ministry from 21st Century Africa*	eds. Benjamin Dean Adriaan Neele
MLD1	*From Cambridge to Colony: Charles Simeon's Enduring Influence on Christianity in Australia*	ed. Edward Loane
MST2	*'Tend My Sheep': The word of God and pastoral ministry*	ed. Keith G Condie

If you have enjoyed this book, you might like to consider

- *supporting the work of the Latimer Trust*
- *reading more of our publications*
- *recommending them to others*

See www.latimertrust.org for more information.

Lightning Source UK Ltd.
Milton Keynes UK
UKOW04f0625300118
317056UK00001B/104/P

9 781906 327446